The Original
COMPUTER
Idiot™

PC User's Guide

for IBM PC's and Compatibles

The Original COMPUTER IDIOT PC User's Guide

Published by

S◆ftMark
2734 Johnson Drive, Suite D
Ventura, CA 93003
(805) 650-5980

ISBN 1-879986-00-0
Printed in the United States of America

10 9 8 7 6 5 4 3 2 1

Distributed in the United States by SoftMark.

For sales inquiries and quantity pricing or for information regarding translations and availability in other countries contact SoftMark at the above address.

Dedication

To the most
inspirational people in my life,
My kids, Nicolas and Alison,
and my Mom. "Hi Mom!"

Acknowledgements

SoftMark would like to thank **Kathryn Lodato** and **Charles Matthews** for their writing and editing contributions, **Chris Martinez** and **Larry White** for their illustration contributions, and **Carrie Dittmar** at MasterPages for her desktop publishing expertise. A special thanks to **Jeanette Lund** for her word processing and editing and proofing skills and suggestions *(solicited and unsolicited)* and of course, all that coffee.

Introduction

You've got The Original COMPUTER IDIOT™ PC User's Guide in your hands. Now, either you've bought it, or someone who thinks you need it got it for you. Your boss, maybe? *Maybe you're the boss,* and you got it for one of your employees. Whatever. This is the book that will make the user computer literate. Simply.

You're not an ***idiot***. As a matter of fact, ***you're probably very smart.*** You just don't know a whole lot about personal computers.

When you hear the term "computer idiot," do you say, "That's me!" *or* "That's someone I know!" Well, you're not alone. There are more computer idiots out there than there are computer literates. It's time to "Just Say No" to computer illiteracy.

With this book in hand, you've taken a positive step towards learning more about the exciting and often *crazy world of computers.* The reality is, people are looking for a simple explanation of computers and we believe this book is that simple explanation.

Our goal is to first, put you at **ease** with computers, then, to put you to **work** with computers. In that order.

The Contents

Chapter 4

Part 2:
Communication

Chapter 5

Chapter 6

Chapter 7

Part 3:
<u>Getting Personal</u>

Chapter 8

Chapter 9

Chapter 10
All About Diskettes

Part 4:
Where All the Fun Begins

Chapter 11
The Software

Chapter 12
Working With Directories

Part 5:
The Rest of the Book

Chapter 1

Your Path to Computer Knowledge

This book is written for the true beginning user. Many beginning users have developed all sorts of phobias towards computers. We've heard most of the stories: everything from pressing the wrong button and blowing up the office to catching a strange machine disease from a computer "virus." *But fear not.* Computers are really quite harmless and we're convinced that you can learn about them.

This book is designed to provide an easy and entertaining way to learn about computers. Overly technical material is kept to a minimum. When we can't avoid the technical, we do our best to put it in terms you can understand. We try to make it as painless as we possibly can.

Your path to computer knowledge will start with the basics: **how to turn the computer on** and **what to do once it starts**. From there we move a little closer, providing more detail with each chapter. By the end of this book, you should have enough knowledge to use your computer without fear.

So... let's stop the small talk and get started. <u>**Good luck!**</u>

The B-A-S-I-C Approach To Learning

Before you enter the world of computers, we want you to know that we assume you know NOTHING about computers. This should take away any pressure you may feel. All you need is an active mind and the right "approach" to succeed in your computer education. We call this approach the **B-A-S-I-C** approach. It's a lot like the way children learn about the world.

A lot of people find it amazing that children can easily learn about computers when it's sometimes difficult for adults. Children naturally follow what we identify as the **B-A-S-I-C** approach to learning. You will be successful in learning about computers if you can use this approach to.

Here's How It Works:

Be Open Minded

RELAX! Don't be afraid of the information.

Approach With Interest

You have to want to learn about computers in order to succeed. "You can bring a horse to water but you can't make him drink."

Study The Material

Learning means studying. There is no way to avoid it. We've tried.

Incorporate The Knowledge

If you don't use your knowledge, you'll lose it. Apply your new knowledge.

Continue Your Education

Build on the information you have learned. Keep up to date with computers.

How We Organized This Book

In this book, we deliberately protect you from technical details until you have enough knowledge to make use of them. We walk you slowly through the information, so that you build your knowledge solidly. Each chapter will help you feel a little more comfortable with the computer.

This book is divided into five parts, each divided into chapters:

Part 1: An Overview of the Personal Computer

Part 1 consists of four chapters that give you an introduction to the world of computers.

Chapter 1 Your Path to Computer Knowledge

Chapter 2 What's a Computer?

Chapter 3 The Basics of Using Your Computer

Chapter 4 The Computer As A System

Part 2: Communication

Part 2 covers how you communicate with the computer and how it communicates with you.

Chapter 5 How The Computer Communicates With You

Chapter 6 How You Communicate With The Computer

Chapter 7 The Proof Is In The Print

Part 3: Getting Personal

Part 3 takes you up close and personal through the insides of the computer, along with diskette information.

Chapter 8 Where It All Happens

Chapter 9 The Computer's Filing Cabinet: Storage Drives

Chapter 10 All About Diskettes

Part 4: Where All the Fun Begins

By the time you get to part 4, you'll have enough knowledge of hardware to start building on your knowledge of software.

Chapter 11 The Software

Chapter 12 Working With Directories

Chapter 13 Working With Files

Part 5: The Rest of the Book

The remaining part of this book consists of tips on buying a computer and a glossary of computer terms.

Chapter 14 Laying Out the Buck$

Glossary (Computer words)

What Do Those Icons (little pictures) Mean?

We use several *icons* and *type styles* in this book to help clarify information. You should be aware of these things while reading.

This little icon indicates that you were supposed to have *learned* something at this point. It regularly appears at the end of each chapter as "**What Did You Learn?**" It also appears when we offer **tips** on this and that.

This little icon is to **remind** you about something we thought was worth reminding you about.

And this little icon is to try to get you to **pay extra special attention** to whatever it is we're talking about.

When we discuss text that appears on the computer monitor, **this is the monitor it'll appear on**. It's just the upper left-hand corner of the monitor, but you get the picture, don't you? To remind you that it's supposed to represent your monitor we label it "Your monitor."

Other times, when working with the software and file sections, you may have to type something on the screen. Everything we want you to type will be indicated in a **bold typeface** on this screen.

When you see type like this on a page, we're trying to bring your attention to certain parts of an illustration. IT IS NOT someone's kid writing in your book.

Chapter 2

What's a Computer?

Computers can be intimidating at first. That's why we start you off slowly, one little step at a time. In this chapter we give a look at the **typical computer system.** You'll read about the basic components of the computer system and learn a little bit about the *history* and *terminology* of computers. After reading this chapter, you should have just enough information to prepare you for later chapters in this book where we go into more details.

The Experts Say

If you looked for a **technical definition** of a computer, you might find something like this:

> *"An electronic apparatus that can receive, process, store and retrieve data, can carry out mathematical and logical operations at high speed and display the results, and can be programmed."*

If you're like most new users, the technical definition may be a mouthful, but nothing you could really sink your teeth into.

Here are **two short facts** about computers:

1) The computer is a stupid machine.
Don't be shocked. It's true. It is an electrical device with only the most primitive capacity for reasoning. A computer can only do what **you** and special instructions, called **software**, tell it to do.

2) A computer only distinguishes between two things: <u>Yes and No</u>.
All the data understood by the computer is either a Yes or a No. With the help of software, the computer can build more complex data from several million Yes and No responses. Eventually this data becomes a letter in a word processing program or a picture in a graphics program. But at the core of the computer's reasoning is merely the ability to distinguish between Yes and No.

Don't worry! Software sweats out this technical stuff for you.

<u>What's In A Name?</u>

Personal computers have been around now for about 12 years. In this time, they have been called by many different names. These names range from the ever popular term, *"PC"*, to the term most often heard after a computer bleeps an error message, "$#*/!".

The computer also has several other names it goes by -

Personal Computer, CPU, Compatible, microcomputer, clone, system - but they all basically refer to the same machine. In this book, we generally refer to the computer as the **"computer."**

<u>They Come in All Shapes and Sizes</u>

There is probably a style of computer for almost every use. Some designs lend themselves to greater portability, while other designs provide more power. Each different "look" has a different name. **All computers have the same basic insides**, but the exterior design determines how a computer will be used. *The following section describes the basic types.*

Desktop

The desktop is probably the most common & popular type of computer. It is typically used on the top of a person's desk, hence the name, desktop. (Pretty original.) All parts of the computer are connected within a central unit. One version of the desktop, called a "slimline computer," has a thinner central unit than the standard desktop.

Tower

The Tower is a personal computer with a vertical or "tower" shape. The Tower has grown in popularity recently with the arrival of uses that require more computing power. (That's because the "box" is bigger and it'll hold more "stuff" inside). Although the Tower can be used by itself, it is frequently used as the controlling system for a whole group, or network, of computers.

Portable Computers

Do you remember the first calculator that was the size of a telephone book? Then, as technology progressed, a calculator ultimately came out that was the size of a credit card. The same thing has happened in the computer world. Standard desktop sized computers have shrunk to the size of a standard loose-leaf notebook. These systems are considered "portable" computers. This allows you to easily carry a computer with you wherever you go.

Laptop

The laptop was the first true portable computer. Since it uses a battery for power, it can be used while traveling by plane or car. It can also be set up in a hotel, home, or office. The laptop got its name from being small enough to fit on, well, your lap. (Another original name.) All components (keyboard, monitor, screen and CPU) for the laptop are contained in one package.

Notebook

The notebook is even smaller than the laptop, the size of a typical, you guessed it, notebook. You know, the same kind of notebook you carried around in high school. The notebook is designed for the same reasons: **Portability**. Computer power on the road.

Back in the "Old Days"

Let's take a step back in history for just a moment so you can see where computers began. When the first electronic computer came out in 1946, it occupied an entire building. It was very heavy, very complicated, and did very little! *The first computer*, called the **E**lectronic **N**umerical **I**ntegrator **A**nd **C**alculator (ENIAC) only had the power of today's pocket calculators. Computers have come a long way since then. Today there are three categories of computers:

Mainframe, Mini, and Personal Computers

Mainframe and Mini Computers are generally used by large corporations for controlling things like manufacturing and development. Personal computers are used in businesses and homes, mainly by individuals like you. **Our focus** will be on **personal computers** (designed for "personal" use). These are computers that conform to the IBM-PC standard.

Several personal computers, designed for the home, were introduced in the 1970's by companies such as Commodore, Apple, Tandy and Atari. It really wasn't until the 1980's, however, when IBM joined the game, that "computer" became a household word. Since then, the world of advanced technology has helped make personal computers *faster, better, cheaper, and easier.* You've picked a good time to learn about these wonderful, time-saving machines.

The Body and Mind of the Computer:

Each part of a computer system can be classified into one of two categories: **Hardware or Software.**

Hardware is the part of the system that you can touch and feel. Hold and carry. It in cludes the central processing unit, monitor, keyboard, mouse, printer, and other hard components of a personal computer. Hard ware is called hardware because it's... yes, hard! Hardware is really the **"body"** of the computer.

Software is the part of the computer that controls the hardware. It consists of previously created instructions that direct the hardware to perform specific tasks, such as word processing. Since it has this **management** capacity, it can be considered the "mind" or knowledge of the computer. Software is the part of the computer system you will interact with most of the time.

There are several different kinds of software available for computers, but as a user, you will only need to know about the two major categories of software: *operating* (**system**) *software* & *applications* (**program**) *software.*

We get into lots more detail about *hardware* and *software* as we progress further into the book.

<u>Compatibility</u>

We told you that computers are made up of hardware and software and that they come in different shapes and sizes. All of these different types of personal computers can be separated into two basic worlds - the IBM world and the Apple world. Each type is named after the major corporation that companies look to for a manufacturing standard. *In this book*, we talk about those computers belonging to *the IBM world.*

You may hear that a computer is "**IBM compatible**." When people are compatible, they get along with each other. It's the same with computers. In order for computers to work together, their parts must be compatible with each other.

"**IBM compatible**" means that the computer and all of its parts are compatible with personal computers built by IBM. IBM is a very large corporation that has built a range of personal computers using certain technology standards. Other companies have followed IBM's standards in developing their hardware and software so they can all communicate together. In other words, they have

What Can It Do For You?

Computers are great with information. They know how to **store** it, how to **add** it, **subtract** it, and generally **process** it. With the help of software, the computer is capable of integrating all of its abilities into ways that benefit you. Listed below are just a few ways computers can help you:

- **Write** letters to friends and relatives.
- **Publish** a newsletter with fancy type styles.
- **Draw** pictures of your dog or cat, or draw house plans.
- **Calculate** your income and expenses for the year.
- **Organize** client lists into sepa- rate groups of information.
- **Play** the latest video games.
- **Learn** how to type faster or teach your child math.
- **Coordinate** all company accounts into an general ledger.
- **Communicate** with other computer users across the country.

And there are many, many more ways to use your computer.

Look Out. It's Hot!

Let's face it. Computers are becoming not only a way to "keep up with the Jones."   They also play a vital role in everyday business. Computers are showing up everywhere: *homes, schools, government, businesses, churches,* and in many other places. With the ability to take you beyond human limitations, a computer can organize, educate, save time, entertain, increase accuracy, and the list goes on. They're hot and here tostay. At least for our lifetime, anyway. **So get use to 'em.**

What Did You Learn?

A computer is a combination of compatible **hardware** and **software** that gives you the ability to do many functions. You can choose from a variety of computer **shapes** and **sizes**, depending on what suits you best.

The *first* computer arrived on the scene in the 1940's and ever since then computers have gotten *smaller*, more *powerful*, and *easier* to use. In the next few chapters you will beginto see the different parts of the typical computer and how those parts work together.

Chapter 3

The Basics of Using Your Computer

"Stick this where?!"

Taking one step closer, we introduce you to a few facts that will get you started using your computer. These include everyday items such as inserting cables correctly and the first thing you see after starting your computer. In later chapters we'll teach you how to work with your computer in more detail.

When you first get a computer system, you may open the box, stand back a little overwhelmed and say, **"How the heck does all this go together?"** RELAX! Take the computer and all of its cables out of the box. *Read the set up instructions* to get help putting it together. We will tell you a few facts in this chapter that might help you get going.

Plugging In

The first thing to remember about computers is that they require electricity for power. Believe it or not, a lot of new computer users can't get their computers started because cables are not plugged in properly.

When you take a look at the **back of the computer**, you will see that almost every socket is shaped differently and there is a matching cable somewhere, just made for that socket. The shape of the socket gives you an idea of which cable plugs into it. ***It's sort of like putting a puzzle together.***

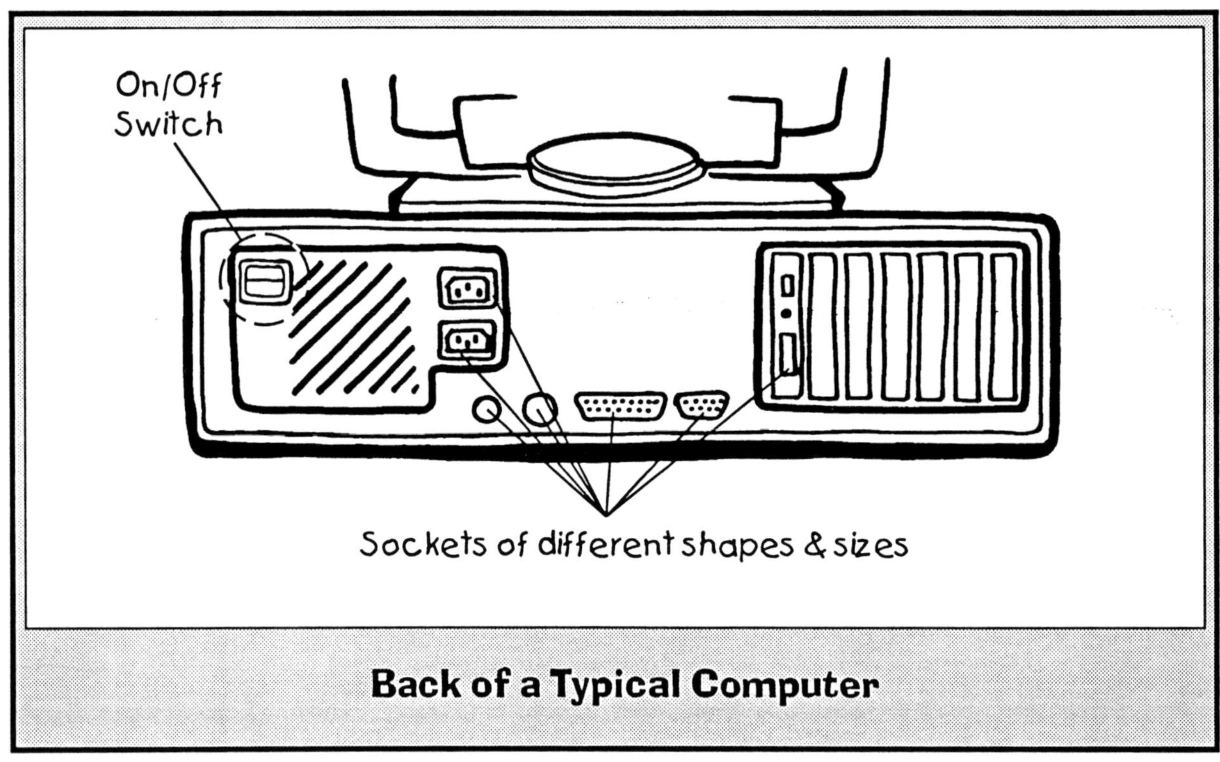

Back of a Typical Computer

The cables that plug into the back of the computer are mainly for **power**, the **monitor**, the **keyboard** and the **printer**.

The following figure shows where these cables are connected:

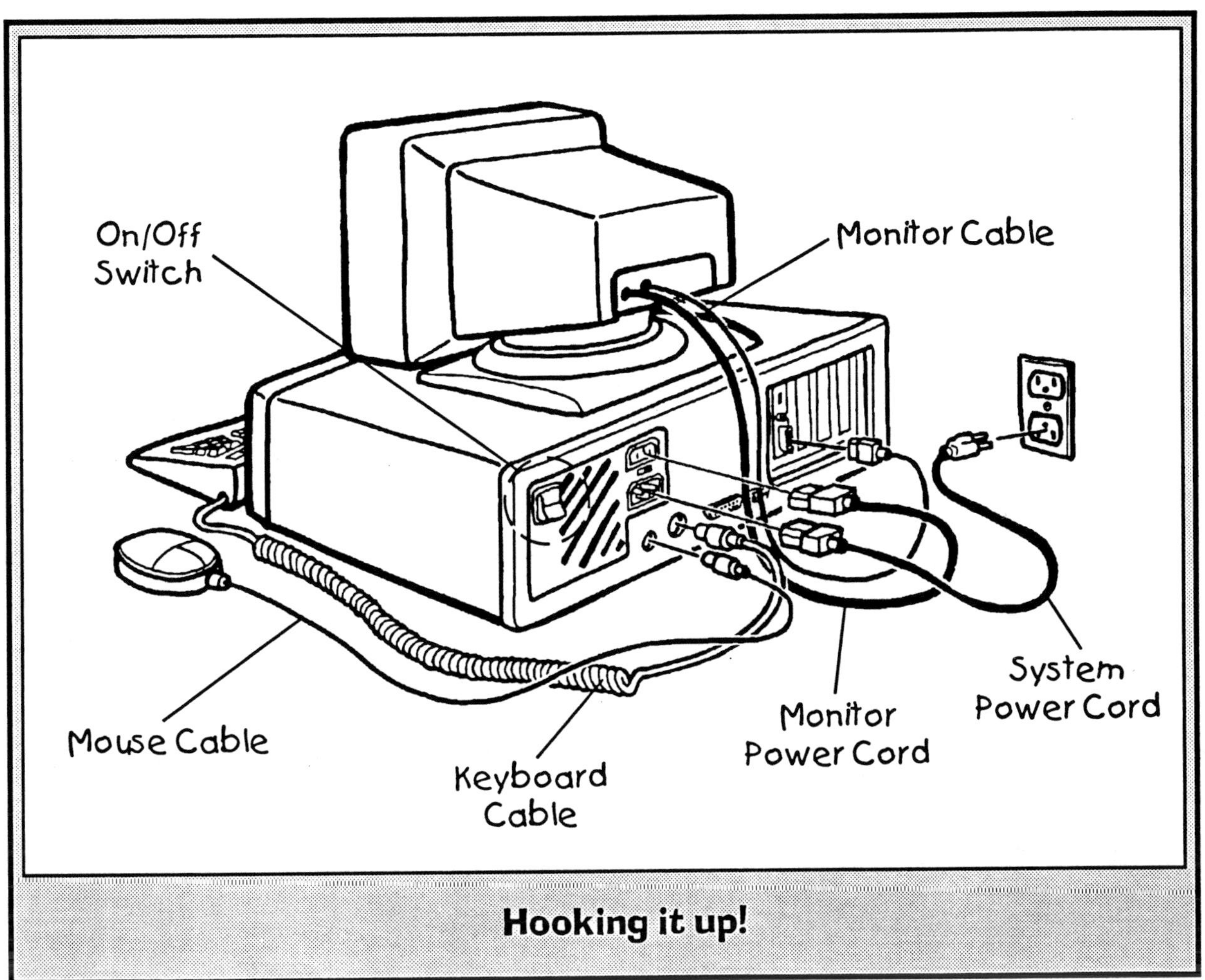

Hooking it up!

System Power Cord

One end of the power cable needs to be plugged into the back of the
computer and the other end should be plugged into a nearby wall socket.
*The end that plugs into the wall socket is simply a standard plug. The
end that plugs into the computer will fit the appropriate socket. You'll
see it.*

Be sure your computer is **OFF**
when working with the power cable.
Electrical shock is not a pleasant experience.

Monitor Cable & Monitor Power Cord

Computer monitors usually have **two** cables. *One cable* plugs directly into the back of the computer and handles all *communication* between the monitor and the main system. This plug is usually rectangular in shape and has several pins. The *other cable* is similar to the main computer power cable. It is the *power cable* for the monitor only.

Keyboard Cable

The keyboard needs to be connected to the main system. If it weren't, then everything you typed would go no further than the keys you press. So, all keyboards have a cable that connects to the back of the computer. The keyboard cable plug is usually round in shape and has 5 pins.

Mouse Cable

The mouse is also hooked up to the main system. Although the mouse is an **optional** thing, it is becoming a very common option among computer users. The mouse also hooks up somewhere in the back of the computer.

Turning the Computer ON

After all cables are plugged in, you need to find the **On/Off switch**. Usually this switch is on the back of the computer in either the right or left hand corner. *Sometimes* it's located on the front or side of the system, all depends on the manufacturer. ***Flip the switch*** to the ON position and presto! **You're ready to start.**

As soon as you flip the switch to the **On position**, the computer does a short self check to get ready for use. You may see a few numbers flash by on your screen. *Don't Panic!* It's just part of the computer's self check. Next, your computer starts the ***Disk Operating System*** (DOS) *software* and prepares itself to start taking orders (commands) from you.

The Disk Operating System (DOS)

Your computer is a machine that requires continuous hand-holding to complete even the simplest of tasks. One tool that helps you guide the computer along is the **Disk Operating System** (DOS) **software**. Most PC computers use DOS as a mediator between you and the computer. DOS commands offer you a very powerful tool in the control of your computer. With DOS you can tell the computer to manipulate information in a variety of ways: *print it, copy it* from one place to another, *erase it, sort it, start a software program* and much more.

DOS *(rhymes with boss)* is the piece of software in the computer that pretty much *controls* everything in your computer. *(Maybe that's why it rhymes so well with boss!)*

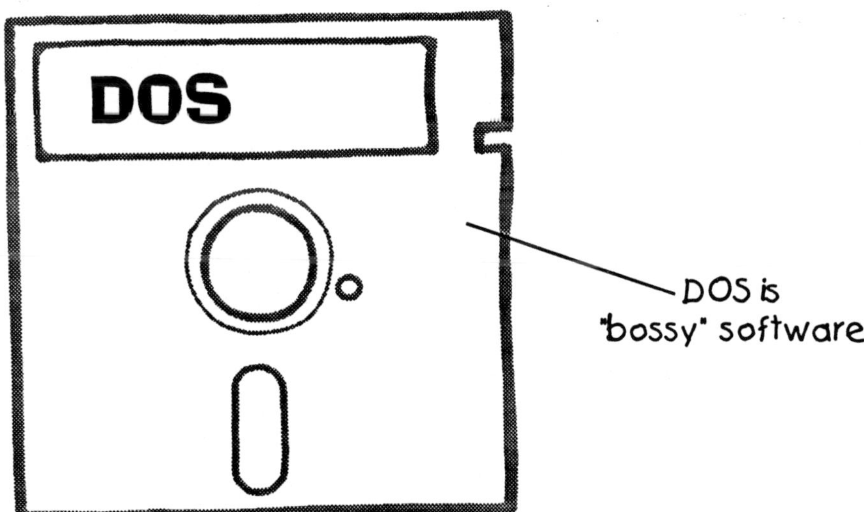

Although we talk about a couple of DOS things in this chapter, **we don't cover DOS in detail here.** However, *Chapters 11, 12 and 13* provide enough information on DOS to get you up and running.

The DOS Prompt

Once DOS is ready, it will display what is called a **"DOS prompt."** The prompt is the operating system's way of telling you, *"Okay I'm ready to take instructions now."* The prompt is a place marker on the computer's screen to show you where information is to be entered next.

The **DOS prompt** looks something like this:

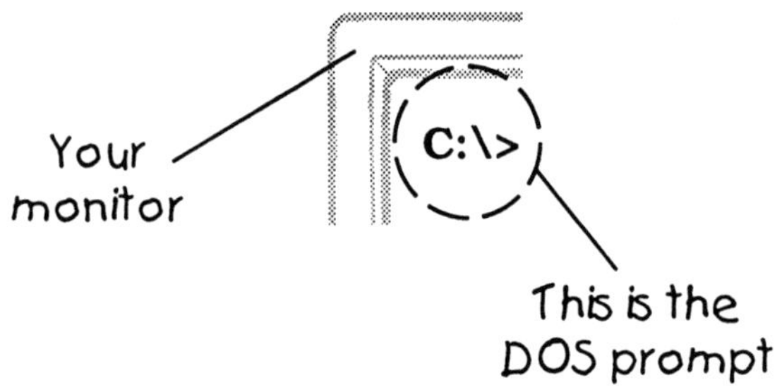

It is made up of a letter (**C**) usually followed by a colon (**:**), a backslash (****) and a greater-than symbol (**>**). Put it all together and it looks like this, **C:\>**. (Sometimes it looks like this: **C>**). The letter itself shows the disk drive that DOS is currently reading. You will most frequently see either of the following two DOS prompts on your screen:

C:\> or A:\>

The "C" prompt signifies that you have access to the main storage disk drive *(the hard drive)* in your system. *The "A" prompt* shows that you access to the secondary storage disk drive *(the floppy disk drive)* on your system.

If you're going to succeed in using your computer, **you must know where your information is located.** The first steps to calm computing is knowing which storage drive you are currently accessing and which drive contains the information you want. You can tell which drive is the current drive simply by looking at the DOS prompt we mentioned earlier. *If your information is on another drive,* it is possible to switch over to that drive.

And that's what we discuss in this next section.

Changing Drives

The DOS prompt that is displayed at system start-up indicates the drive you are accessing. But, you don't have to stick that drive. Assume that the "C" prompt was displayed when you turned the computer ON. Now you want to look at the information that is on drive "A." You need to change the current drive from "C" to "A."

To change the drive, you simply type the name of the drive you want to change to and follow it with a colon (:). For example, to access the information in the "**A**" drive while still in the "**C**" drive, you would *type*: **A:** at the current prompt.

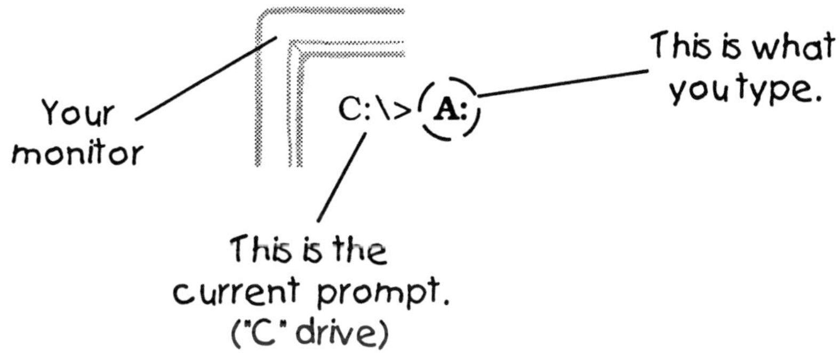

and then press the key marked **ENTER**.
The system prompt will change to:

       A:\>

Try it. Does it work? Yup!

The steps for *changing the current drive* are easy. Here they are at a glance:

1) **Note** which drive you are in and which drive you want to access.

2) Type the **drive letter** you want to access. (**A,B.C,** etc.)

3) Type a **Colon** (:)

4) Press the **ENTER** key.

Yeah! You have just learned your **first** DOS command. *Be proud!* Go around and show your friends!

What's a Cursor?

Next to the prompt you will see a **flashing dash** symbol. This symbol or marker, is called a cursor. It tells you where the next command or piece of information will be entered. Therefor, it is important to know the cursor's location.

There will always be some type of cursor on the screen to show you where you are. Although a cursor is typically a flashing dash symbol, *each software program may customize the shape of the cursor to best suit that software program.* A cursor can take the shape of an **arrow, square,** **underline**, etc. You'll know when you see it. *Trust me.*

24

You can move the cursor around on the screen by using the keys on the keyboard that have arrows on them. These are called *arrow keys* or *cursor control keys*. We will talk more about these keys and the keyboard in Chapter 6.

Oh $#*!!   Did I Touch the Wrong Button?

The biggest fear many beginners have is destroying information or *breaking the computer* by pressing the wrong key. The truth is that neither is easy to do. *No one key* on the keyboard is capable of doing irreparable damage to your system. Most commands that will **erase** or **delete** information are usually followed by a prompt (question) on the screen asking if you are sure you want to continue with the command.

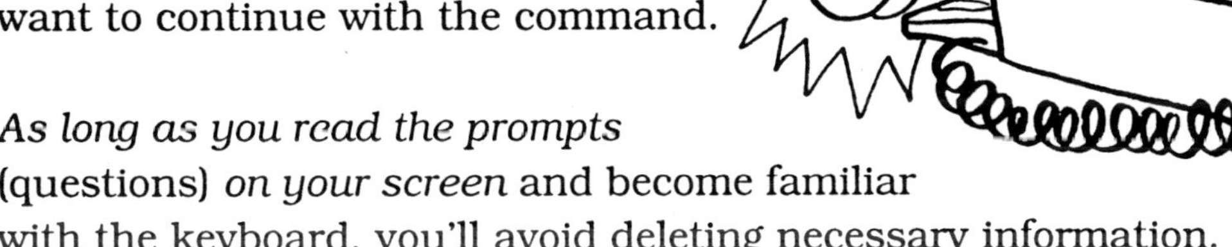

As long as you read the prompts (questions) *on your screen* and become familiar with the keyboard, you'll avoid deleting necessary information.

Error Messages

There will be times when you either enter a command incorrectly, or the computer has a problem, or the software has a problem. Many times, these problems result when the computer cannot complete a task. *Even the best of us encounter these situations.*

When there is a problem, the computer will display an ***error message*** on the monitor. These messages are typically preceded by a "*beep*" sound from the computer. (We've heard some people say they think the "*beep*" is the computer saying "*Ouch! That hurt!*" But we all know that computers aren't alive, *don't we?*) An error message is the computers way of telling you that something is wrong and it won't be able to complete a command.

Have no fear, many error messages sound worse than they really are. Software programmers often use scary words like "*invalid,*" "*insufficient,*" and "*bad command*" when a computer cannot complete a function. **Don't let these words intimidate you**. You won't be taken off to jail for issuing a "bad command." The error may be as simple as *mis-typing* a DOS command name. So don't panic. In that case, **look at what you typed**. You may be able to see the problem.

Here's an error message for you:
Insufficient disk space.
It means the disk is full. There isn't room on the disk to copy or create anymore files.

What happened? You tried to put too many files on that disk. You fed it too much! **The cure?** Alka-Seltzer? No. Delete some files or copy them to another disk.

Full Disk!

Most error messages are self explanatory. (Ha-Ha!) If you have a question, you should refer to your DOS or software manual for further clarification.

When in doubt, read your manual. Most people try to avoid this at all costs, but it really is the best place to turn for help. It may require some searching, but manuals usually contain the answers to most computer user questions.

Remember to Save Your Information

Probably the easiest way to lose valuable information and hours of hard work *is to forget to save it.* When you have finished using a software program on your computer, there is an important thing to remember:

Save your work!
Make sure you have saved all of your work to a disk drive for permanent storage **before** you turn the power off.

All of the information that you have **NOT** saved to your storage disk drive (i.e., hard drive or floppy drive) **will be erased** once you turn off the system. Each software program will have a different command for saving information. *Be sure to learn the correct way to save your work in each software program that you use.*

Re-Starting Your Computer

There may come a time when you want to restart your computer. For example, when you make changes to your system setup or when your computer will not accept any input through the keyboard. When you do restart your computer what you are doing is *"re-booting."* Re-booting is the ability to restart your computer without turning the power to the computer off and on again. *It's not healthy* for your computer to be constantly turned off and on by the power switch, so re-booting comes in handy. Here's two ways to reboot:

    1) Press the **Ctrl, Alt,** and **Del** keys all at the same time.

    2) Press the **Reset** button on the front panel or side of your computer.

We do not advise re-booting too often. It is normally used as a last resort, when you've tried to get your computer unstuck through all other means. Also, re-booting will erase any information that has not been saved to your storage drive, just as it does when you turn your computer off.

What Did You Learn?

You have now had your *first introduction* to what it is like to use a computer. Go through a system check list before start ing your computer. This check list will include attaching all cables and turning the computer ON.

Once turned on, the *Disk Operating System* (DOS) takes over and gives you a *system prompt*. This prompt tells you what drive you are accessing. The *cursor* shows you where your next command will be entered.

Error messages tell you when the computer is unable to perform an operation. When you are unable to operate your computer, you may have to *restart* it using a reboot method. You should always *remember to save* your information to a storage drive before turning your computer off.

The Computer As A System

In this book, we describe the separate pieces that make up a whole computer system. The monitor. The keyboard. The printer. The processor chip. The floppy disk drive. The hard disk drive. The operating system. Application software. Yes, believe it or not, you'll learn about all of these.

They are not the "handful" you may think they are! In reality, these parts do not act individually. They all communicate and interact with each other. And in many cases these parts also interact with you, the computer user.

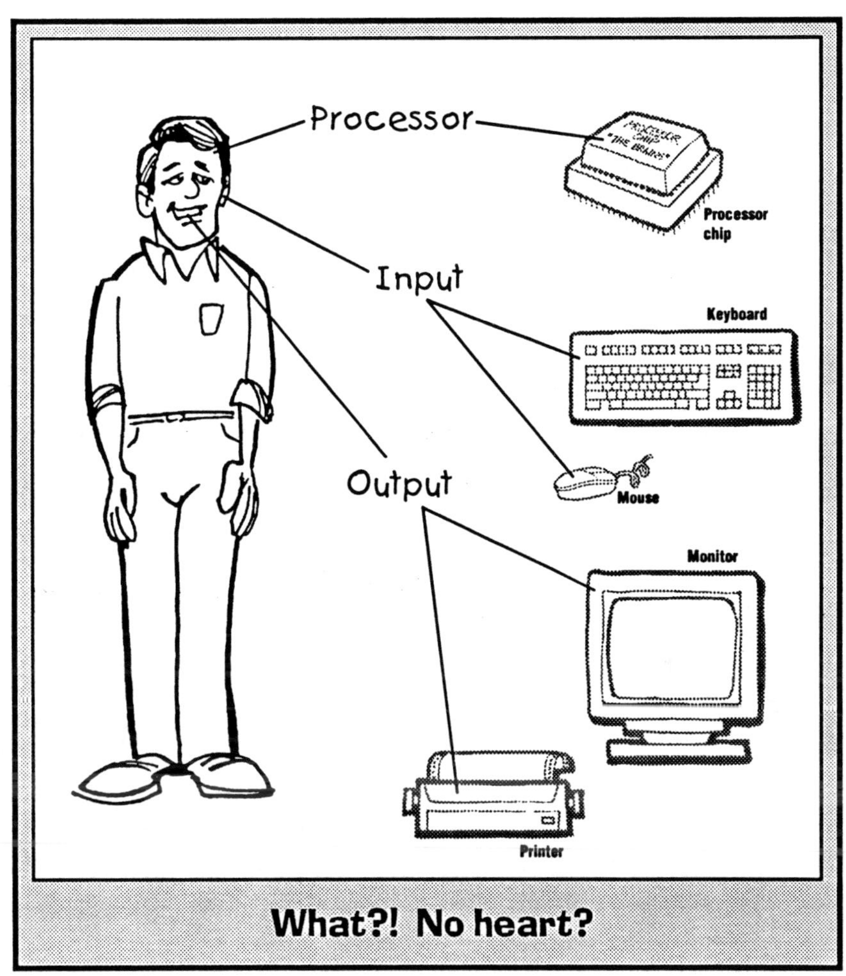

It's Almost Like a Person

As with people, computers come in all shapes and sizes, yet they all have the same basic parts. All computers communicate with you through monitor screen, system lights and printers. And the computer receives information from you through its keyboard. It even has a brain to analyze and process the information it receives. In fact, your computer even remembers all the information you enter. The following shows the various parts of a computer and what their human equivalents would be:

Like your body, the parts of a computer work together as a system. Electricity powers the main parts of a computer. And the various parts of the system communicate which each other by transferring small pieces of information, called bits, to one another.

Data and Cables

Computer bits (data) flow through **cables** and along **circuits** within the computer. If you were to see a bit, it wouldn't seem like much. But when you combine many of these small pieces of data together, you get instructions for making information, moving boxes on the screen, and even making sounds.

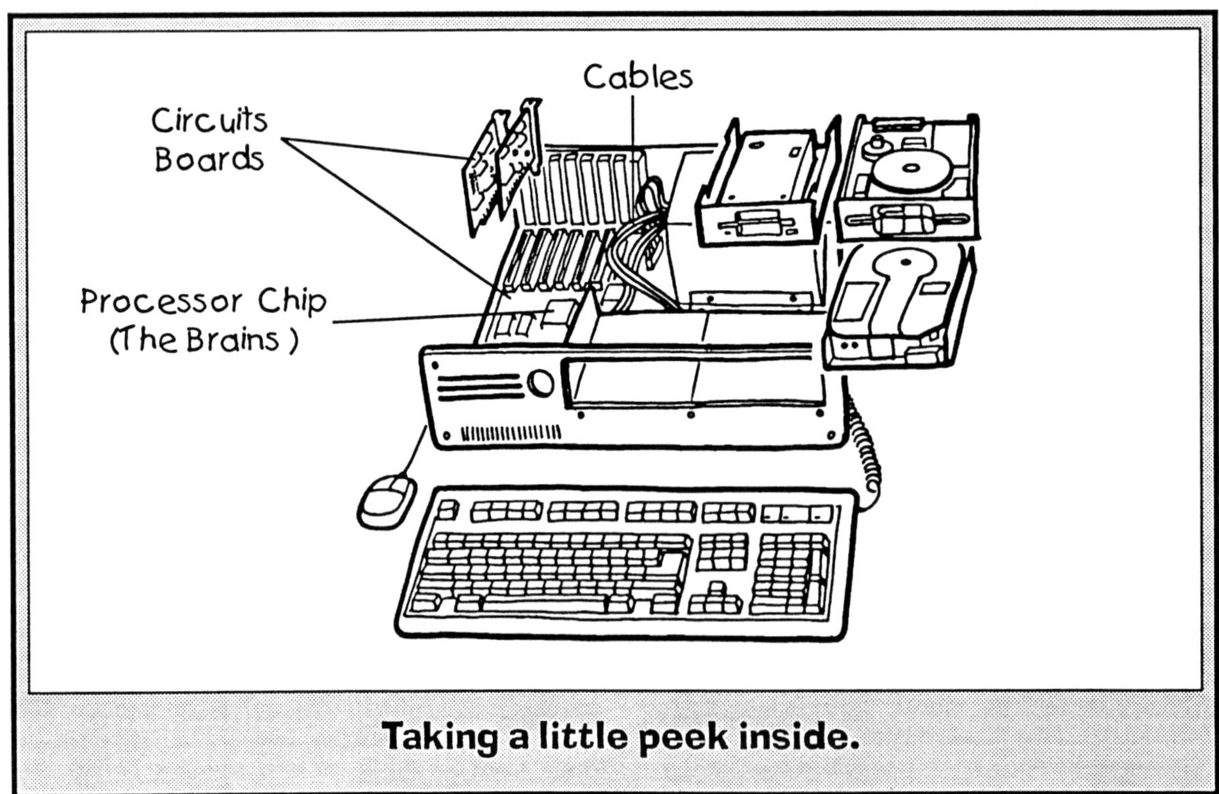

Taking a little peek inside.

Thousands and thousands of bits are transferred along computer cables. So it's surprising that a computer can keep track of all this data. *But it doesn't happen magically.* Each and every computer has a central director, called the **processor chip** (the Brains), that directs the movement of the data among the various parts of the system, sort of like a traffic cop. If the different parts of a computer got paid a salary for their jobs, the processor chip would be the highest paid guy in the company.

The Central Brain

The **processor chip** takes information from one part, say your **keyboard**, and pushes it through the system until it ends up in another place, say your monitor. So, if you've ever wondered what is responsible for translating your *keyboard* typing into real words that appear on the screen, now you know it's the *processor chip*.

"Hey! Can you process this letter, please?"

The processor chip usually lies on the main system board. This board sits inside the body of your computer. When working with a computer, you usually will not see the system board, processor chips, and various storage drives. It is in this main area, sometimes referred to as the *Central Processing Unit* (CPU), where all of the "real" computing is done. We go into detail on this subject in Chapter 8.

What Did You Learn?

Your computer system contains individual parts responsible for separate and unique functions. Some parts **process** information, some **save** information, and others **communicate** information to you, the computer user. To complete the work you want, these parts must *work together as a system*, much like the human body.

In later chapters we will investigate each part of the computer what they look like, what they do, and how you work with them.

Chapter 5

How The Computer Communicates With You

Now that you have been introduced to the computer, it is important to know how you can communicate with each other. In this chapter, we tell you about *one* of the ways a *computer communicates with you.*

You will not see the inside of the computer while using it. The insides of your computer do not tell you much about the letter you are writing while using the computer. You will find yourself spending most of the time looking at the **computer monitor** screen.

The computer is communicating with you by **showing you** the **words** you type, the **pictures** you draw, and the **numbers** you enter. It may sometimes ask you questions and give you information.

The computer itself does not require the monitor to do its job. However, it must use the monitor to *communicate with you.* Like other parts in a computer system, monitors come in various types. When choosing a monitor, you'll want to be careful in choosing the type that suits your needs. Since the time you spend on a computer is also spent looking at the monitor, you will want one that is right for you.

What is a Monitor?

The monitor is the thing you're looking at when you use your computer. *A monitor looks and acts a lot like a television set.* It has a screen and control dials that allow you to adjust the brightness and contrast of the picture. The monitor can also display words (text and numbers) and pictures (graphics). Picture quality on the television still exceeds computer monitor quality. But not by much; computer monitor quality is catching up fast.

> You may hear **several different names** used for computer monitors such as; **monitor, screen, display, terminal, CRT** (cathode ray tube), **VDT** (video display terminal), **LCD** (liquid display terminal).

Computer monitors come in a variety of **sizes.** They also come in **color** and **monochrome** models. In addition, you can choose the **resolution,** or picture quality, of the screen you purchase.

Monitor Sizes

Monitors come in different. Like T.V.'s sets, they are measured by the diagonal height of the screen - from the bottom left corner of the screen to the upper right corner. Monitors selling today are 12-inch, 14-inch, 19-inch, and 20-inch in size. They keep getting bigger too. The most popular monitor purchased today is the 14-inch monitor.

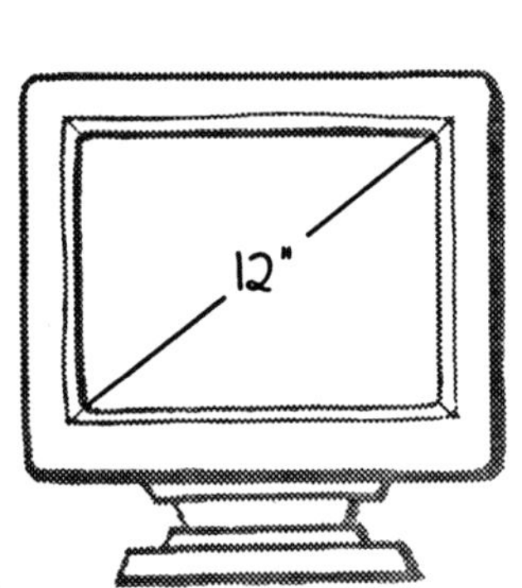

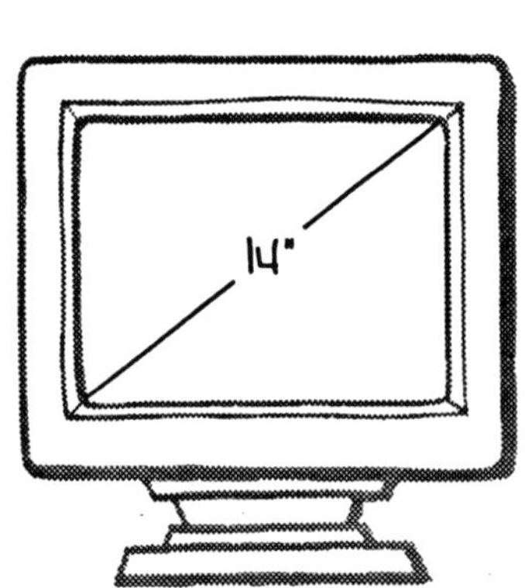

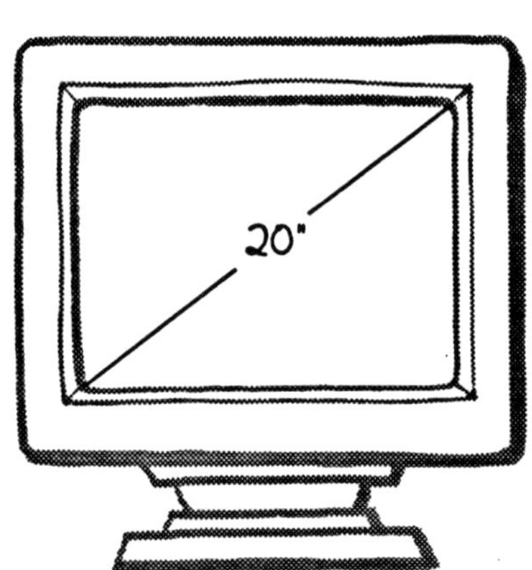

Regardless of its size, a monitor will typically display 25 lines of informa
tion on its screen. So larger screens often show larger text. Some special
monitors will show a full page consisting of 55 lines, or two pages, of
information. These special monitors are usually purchased for use with a
specific type of software.

Color or Monochrome

There are two basic types of televisions: black & white and color. Computer monitors are similar; except the black & white version is referred to
as "**monochrome.**" When personal computers first took off, most people
used a monochrome monitor. These monochrome monitors showed
green or amber words and graphics on a black background. Monochrome monitors display text, numbers, and some graphics in varying
shades of one color. There are also some monochrome monitors that
have a paper white background with black and gray text and graphics.

Now, with technology advances, more application software uses *color* capabilities. Color monitors display text and graphics in full color. The range of colors
and the quality of the screen depend on the software and hardware supporting
the monitor. We will cover the supporting equipment in this section.

What Are the Possibilities?

All monitors are not created equal. Each monitor will have certain capabilities
that depend on its supporting equipment. First a monitor will have either
monochrome or **color** capabilities.

Then there is the **quality** of what you see on the screen. This quality is usually
measured in terms of *resolution,* or the number of dots available to the images
on the screen. Every character and image on the screen is composed of hundreds of small dots called *pixels.* The *more dots available per square inch,* the
smoother and sharper the images.

The **resolution**, or quality, of what you see on the screen, is partly determined by the electronic board plugged inside the computer. This board is referred to as the "*video card*".

Video Card

The video card is a piece of equipment that helps determine monitor resolution. The video card, sometimes referred to as the "*video adapter board*", is an **electronic circuit board** that goes **inside** your computer. It allows communication between the computer and the moni tor and determines some of the capabilities of the moni tor. Both the monitor and the video card, as a team, create the quality of what you see.

The four main types of video cards for color monitors, from least to most expensive, are called **CGA** (color graphics adapter), **EGA** (en hanced video adapter), **VGA** (video graphics array) and **SuperVGA** (super video graphics array). Monochrome monitors use a video card for text only *or* for text and graphics.

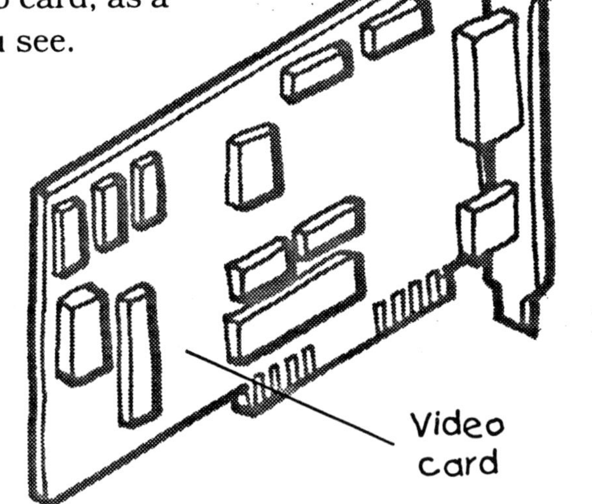

<u>Types of Display Screen Quality</u>: *Monochrome*

There are *three* main types of display quality available for **monochrome** monitors:

Text only

Displays only *letters* and *numbers* in the color of your monitor. It limits your use because it will not work with software that uses graphics.

Text and Graphics

Displays text, graphics, *drawings, diagrams,* and *pictures* in mono-chrome color (one color).

Video Graphics Array

Shows both *text* and *graphics* in **top quality**. Systems with a VGA screen need a *VGA card* (board) installed.

Types of Display Screen Quality: *Color*

There are several types of display quality for color monitors. As you move up in quality, from **CGA** to **EGA** to **VGA** to **SuperVGA** to **PGA** and **XGA**, you will also see an *increase in price.* But the price differences have decreased in recent years. So it's almost worth it to go for higher quality.

CGA (Color Graphics Adapter)

A CGA setup is the **lowest** level you can obtain on a color monitor. It will display both text and graphics. However, you can usually tell a CGA screen from across the room. Its images have a "staircase look" where the edges are very jagged and unsmooth. In terms of resolution, the dots on the screen are farther apart. *The CGA adapter card can only be used with a CGA monitor.*

EGA (Enhanced Graphics Adapter)

EGA is a **step up** in quality from the CGA. It can display both text and graphics. When you look at an EGA screen, you may see some rough edges on graphic images, but they are not nearly as apparent as on the CGA screen. *An EGA adapter card can only be used with an EGA Monitor.*

VGA (Video Graphics Array)

VGA is **almost** *the best* quality you can get with a color monitor. VGA screens will get you pretty darn close to T.V. Screen resolution. These screens show both text and graphics. One of the growing uses of the

VGA screen is with video images. A VGA quality screen is required for such sophisticated software as animation and multimedia (use of text, graphics, and video together on screen.) software. *You can use a VGA card with either a VGA color or VGA monochrome monitor.*

SuperVGA (Super Video Graphics Array)

An enhanced version of the VGA card. Our recommended **best** buy. Called the *"SuperVGA,"* the SuperVGA card handles everything that a normal VGA card can, but it offers an even higher screen quality. *Also costs a little more but worth it.*

PGA (Professional Graphics Adapter)
XGA (Extended Graphics Adapter)

That' right! **Better** than the SuperVGA and... **costs alot more.** Used by professional types that are using fancy, expensive and advanced software. Save your money.

Here's A Tip!

If you want a color monitor, ask what the price difference is between a **VGA** and **SuperVGA** monitor. These days it may not cost much more for a SuperVGA setup and the quality is much better. **We *do not* recommend** the CGA or EGA monitors due to their low screen quality. (Don't think they make 'em anymore.)

If you are getting a VGA or Super VGA monitor to do extensive graphics and drawings, you should talk to your dealer about how much **memory** is on the video adapter card. Extensive graphics *require* more video adapter memory. Most VGA adapter cards come with 256 kilobytes of memory *(we'll explain what memory is in later chapters)* but you may need to upgrade to 512 kilobytes or 1 megabyte.

Also, remember that you must have a video card for the computer to communicate with the monitor. ***Make sure the card is included the quote for the monitor you are interested in.***

What Did You Learn?

The computer monitor is something you have to look at *every time* you use your computer. Make sure you like the quality you see. Ask yourself: Is the text clear and crisp to read? Is the color easy on your eyes? Will it work with your computer and software?

The **quality** of computer screens can vary from monitor to monitor. It is important that you understand the choices you have when buying a monitor. When you visit a computer dealer, have him show you the differences in the various screen qualities. Monitors come in several screen **sizes**, have the capabilities for **color** or **monochrome** displays, and can show graphic images in **CGA, EGA, VGA** and **SuperVGA** quality. (**PGA** and **XGA** is too expensive!)

A *monochrome* monitor is best for working with numbers and text. If this is your computer's main function, then a monochrome monitor may be your best buy. *Color* monitors are excellent for graphics and game applications. *They also liven up the time you spend using your computer.* Color monitors will cost more than monochrome monitors, but in the long run, you will probably be much happier.

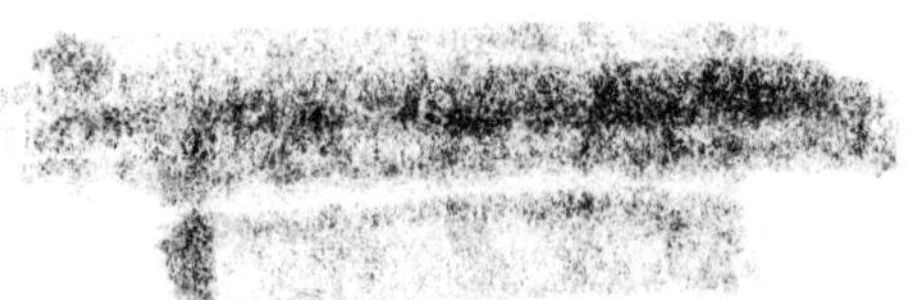

Chapter 6

How You Communicate With The Computer

We all know how to shake hands and say "hello." But how do you communicate with something that doesn't have hands or a mouth and doesn't understand any human language you speak to it? From the last chapter, you know how the computer expresses itself - *through the monitor.* Now, you ask, **"How do I express myself so that the computer can understand?"**

This handless, mouthless, kind of dumb creature may sound like an alien from space. Unfortunately aliens and your computer have a few things in common. So, you need to find alternative ways to communicate with your computer.

Since computers do not understand the spoken language *yet,* you need to use special tools. These tools, called a **keyboard** and a **mouse**, are your primary way of interacting with the computer. Without them you would remain forever speechless in the "eyes" of your computer.

The keyboard will appear familiar to you. It resembles the keys you see on a standard typewriter and functions much the same. It also has some special keys for software-specific instructions. The keyboard, you will find, *is your main way* of giving the computer instructions and information.

The mouse is a communication tool that is gaining in popularity. Many new software programs take advantage of the mouse's *unique features*. The mouse, with its long plug-in cord, allows you to **point** and choose computer commands from menus and boxes on the screen instead of typing in instructions through the keyboard. Most people find the mouse especially useful when working with *graphical software packages*. It gives you the ability to draw and interact with the computer more easily.

In this chapter, we will use examples to illustrate the most common uses of the keyboard and mouse. *The sections in this chapter can also be used as a **reference*** for the two communication devices.

The Keyboard

The keyboard is a *standard* part of all computers. It is also the most familiar to beginners because it looks so much like a typewriter. In this section, we will discuss the different keys on the keyboard. We use the keyboard called a **"101 keyboard"** as our example. It gets its name from the number of keys it contains - 101 (pretty clever, don't you think?) It is the most widely used keyboard 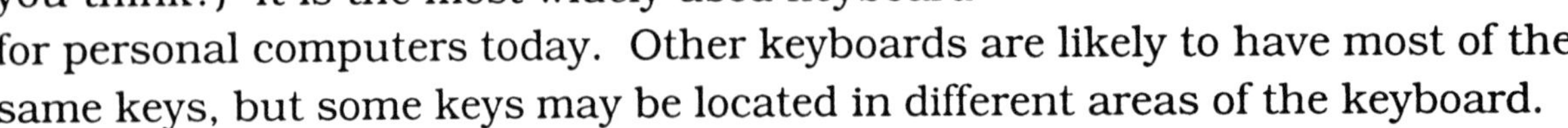 for personal computers today. Other keyboards are likely to have most of the same keys, but some keys may be located in different areas of the keyboard.

Many beginners are afraid that they may press the wrong key on their keyboard and they'll break the system. But in reality, no one key on the keyboard can do irreparable damage to your computer. The best way to avoid pressing the wrong key is to fully understand the keyboard and what each key can do. That is why we dedicate most of this chapter to *understanding the keyboard.*

The Major Sections on the Keyboard

In this section we'll discuss the main sections of your keyboard.

Letter and Number Keys (Typewriter Key Area)

The main section of the key board is the most familiar to people because it is laid out like a standard typewriter keyboard. You use the alphabet and number keys to type in commands and information.

Function Keys (Labeled F1 thru F12)

The top row of the keyboard con sists of function keys that act as 

shortcut keys. Thcy are marked from **F1** to **F12**. These keys perform specific functions with one keystroke rather than what can sometimes take many keystrokes. *(These keys may also appear in two columns to the left side of some older keyboards.)*

Cursor Control Keypad

The cursor control keypad consists of keys that give you control over the cursor. (Remember that the cursor is the *flashing dash symbol* that acts as a marker of where the next typed char-acter will appear.) These keys include directional arrows that allow you to move the cursor around the screen and through an information file. These keys are most often used in text editing.

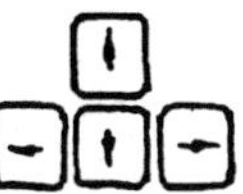

Numeric Keypad

The numeric keypad has a **dual** purpose. The *primary* purpose is similar to a calculator or a 10-key machine with numbers and mathematical symbols. The *secondary* purpose gives you control over the cursor (kindof a backup cursor keypad). You'll see the same arrow keys on the numeric keypad as you saw on the cursor control keypad area.

LED's (Light Emitting Diodes)

Notice the **"lights"** on the keyboard? These lights are called LED's or *Light Emitting Diodes*. The LED's on the keyboard tell you that a specific key function is working when the light is *on* and NOT working when the light is *off*. These little lights can be found on the keyboard display panels or *on the keys themselves*. They usually give off a green or red glow (light) but have been known to appear in other colors. You will generally find an LED indicator for the **Caps Lock, NumLock** and **Scroll Lock** keys on the keyboard. We discuss each of these keys in the next section.

All the Boards Keys: A Closer Look

In the following section, we take a closer look at each of the sections on the keyboard. You should note that ***the action of each of these keys is performed at the present position of the cursor.*** After you press a key, the cursor will move to the new position.

Each key or set of keys is described here and, where appropriate, an example using that key is given. We use the same example throughout this section - *a letter to your Aunt Shirley.*

Letter and Number Keys (Typewriter Key Area)

Enter key

This key is **really** important. Most computer keyboards have *two of these keys*. They both work identically. A *second enter ke* is placed by the numeric keypad to help with the rapid entry of numbers. The Enter key may be labeled as *"Enter"*, *"Return"* or it might just be a *long left pointing arrow.*

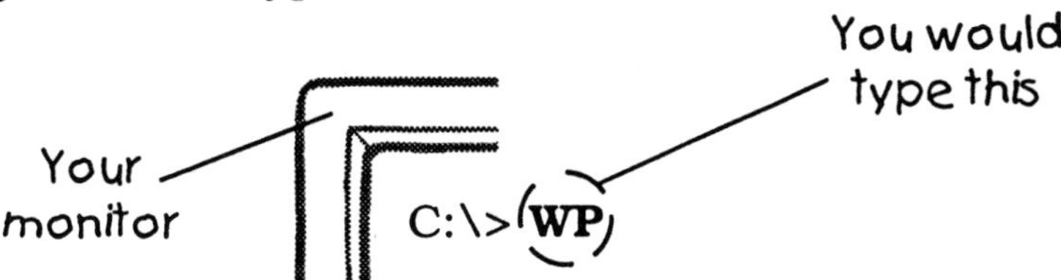

When you press the Enter key, *you're telling the computer to perform the command you just typed.* The computer waits for you to press the Enter key to confirm that **"Yes"** you want it to do what you just told it to do

The Enter key also works like the *carriage return* on a typewriter. For example, it marks the end of a paragraph or line and then moves down to the next line in a word processing program. For this reason, it is called the Return key on some keyboards. We will just stick with calling it "the Enter key".

> ***Example.*** The first thing you do before starting a program is to type a command at the DOS prompt. For example, to start WordPerfect, a popular word processing program, you would type **"WP"**.

But just typing "WP" will not get you very far. All commands entered at the prompt **must** be followed by a stroke to one very important key - ***the Enter key.*** In this case, you need to press Enter after typing "WP." That way the computer knows that you want to start the WordPerfect program.

Letter and Number keys

The main part of the keyboard consists of letters of the **alpha-bet, numbers,** and **symbol keys.** Most of these keys will be familiar to you because they look like the keys on a typewriter. They are white in color and you'll find these keys laying around the center of the keyboard.

> ***Example.*** After entering the WordPerfect program, you will have a *blank screen.* On this screen, you can begin typing a letter to your Aunt using the **letter keys** in the main section of the keyboard.

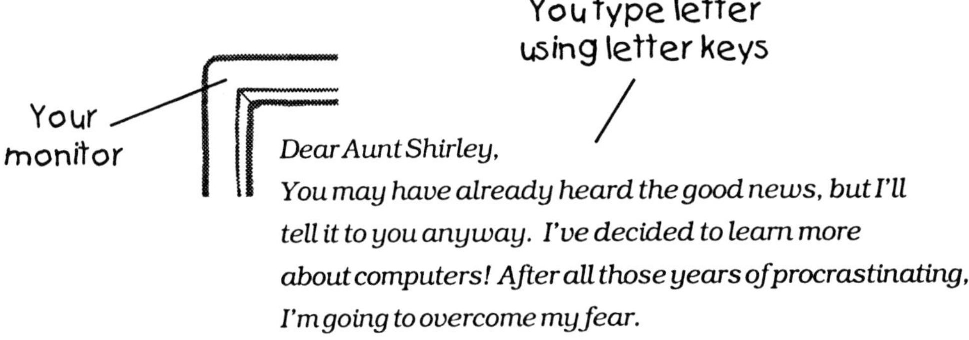

Shift key

The Shift key allows you to ***type capital letters*** and the ***symbols*** shown above the numbers on your keyboard. Just hold the Shift key down while you press the letter or number key. Again, the Shift key functions like its counterpart on the typewriter.

> ***Example.*** In the first part of your letter you had to use the Shift key to capitalize the first letter of each sentence. As you continue the letter, you press the Shift key again to type "I" as the first letter of the next sentence:

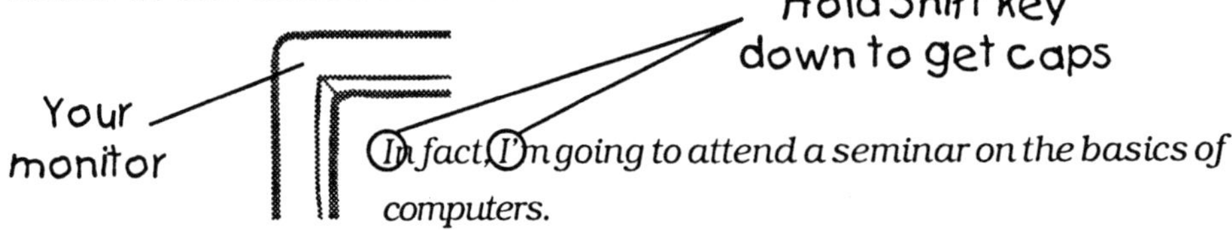

Caps Lock key

When you press the Caps Lock key once, it will type all 26 letters of the alphabet in capital letters until you press it again. **Unlike** the Shift key, you do not have to hold the Caps Lock key down to get the capital letters. When you press on the Caps Lock key, you will note that the LED light for the Caps Lock turns ON. The **LED** *(light)* **is ON** when you are in *Caps Lock mode.*

Note that you will **still need to press** the Shift key to obtain the symbols above the numbers. The Caps Lock key **does not affect** the number row of keys. This is the *only difference* between the Caps Lock key and the Shift Lock key on a typewriter.

Example. While starting the next paragraph of your letter to Aunt Shirley, you *unknowingly* stumble across the Caps Lock key:

I GUESS EVERYONE THOUGHT I'D BE THE LAST TO LEARN ABOUT... WAIT A SECOND AUNT SHIRLEY I THINK MY SHIFT KEY IS STUCK. YOU'LL HAVE TO EXCUSE ALL OF MY CAPITALIZING. A LITTLE LIGHT ON TOP OF MY KEYBOARD JUST TURNED ON TOO. I GUESS I HAVEN'T LEARNED ALL THERE IS TO KNOW ABOUT A COMPUTER KEYBOARD YET.

And right you will be. You hold the Shift key down to type a letter in capital form. But to type many letters in capital form, you press down the **Caps Lock** key.

Tab key

The Tab key is a cursor positioning key that advances the cursor to the next tab stop *(a column position within your screen)*. The Tab key moves your cursor quickly to predefined locations on a line. It's similar to a Tab key on a typewriter. The cursor will indicate where a tab has moved to. The cursor moves to the **right** *(forward)* if the **Tab key is pressed.** It will move to the **left** *(backward)* if you **hold the SHIFT key down while pressing the Tab key.** Usually there are arrows on the TAB key that indicate the direction the cursor will move.

Backspace key

The Backspace key is really the "***backwards delete***" key. It moves the cursor one space to the left (backward) and deletes any letters or numbers in its way. You should note the difference between this key and the Delete key, which is located on the Cursor Control Keypad. ***The Backspace key has an arrow on it and it deletes the letter or number to the left of the cursor.*** The Delete key deletes the character at the cursor's location.

Space bar

The space bar will put an empty space where it is used. This bar works like the one you find on a typewriter. Some users often *overuse* the space bar as a way of indenting text. You should rely on the space bar to **create space between words** and the Tab key to indent text.

Ctrl key

The Ctrl (short for Control) key is used concurrently with other keys to perform a certain software function. For example, when you press Ctrl and the F7 function key at the same time while in a word processing software program, you are sending your work to a printer for printing. ***Your software manual should tell you the specific function*** of the Ctrl key as used with that software. You'll find one each below the Shift keys. They both work the same.

Alt key

The Alt (short for Alternate) key, like the Ctrl key, *is also used with other keys* to complete software functions. You can find one on each side of the space bar (on Enhanced keyboards.) Like the Ctrl key, it doesn't matter which Alt key you press.

Function Keys (Labeled F1 thru F12)

Function keys

Function keys are the keys that are labeled *F1 thru F12.* You'll find these keys at the *top of the keyboard,* in a row, on the enhanced 101 keyboard or, *on "older" keyboards,* you'll find the F1 through F10 keys on the left-hand side of the keyboard. (No mistake, there were only 10 function keys on the earlier keyboards.)

These keys are assigned different functions, depending on the software program that is currently loaded. *For example,* F1 may be a request for help in one software program, while F1 may be a request to print a document on another software program. Make sense? Also... *These keys are used in combination with the* **Shift, Ctrl, Alt keys** in some software programs to provide even more functions. These keys can be thought of as *"shortcut"* keys.

Esc key

Esc is short for the word **"escape."** In some programs this key allows you to "undo" your last keystroke. Many times this key be comes your best friend. While using a some software programs, pressing Esc allows you to **back track** through your steps and *undo* any un wanted changes you may have made. You can learn what this key will do *specifically* in each software program by reading your software manual. This key can usually be found in the upper left-hand corner of the enhanced keyboard in the function key row.

Cursor Control Keypad

Arrow keys

Each arrow key indicates the **direction** in which the cursor will move when that key is pressed. *Ain't it great when the function of the key is so obvious?* The arrows keys are useful for navigating through files. For example, in a word processing program you can move quickly through lines of text by using the arrow keys.

> *Example.* Let's say that you wanted to jump to the end of the letter to your Aunt Shirley to finish it. Your cursor is still in the middle of the letter, so to get down to the bottom of the letter, you repeatedly press the arrow key that points down until you reach the end of the letter. Easy!

Insert key

The Insert key allows you to toggle *(go On and Off)* between either inserting information or typing over information. When Insert is **ON** you can *insert new information* and existing information will move over to the right of your cursor. When Insert is **OFF**, you will *type over and replace* the existing information.

Delete key

The Delete key *removes* the character at the cursor's current location. This key is also used in conjuction with the Ctrl and Alt key to "re-boot" or restart your computer. (See Re-Starting Your Computer, Chapter 3.)

Home key

The Home key **moves the cursor** to the top left hand corner of the  screen or the top of the file on which you are working. *The function of this key could depend on the software you are using.* You can consider this key as returning you to your point of origin, or "home." In this case, that point is the beginning of the screen or document on which you are working.

> **_Example._** At the end of your letter, you could easily move to a sentence near the beginning of the letter. You would *first press* the Home key and then move down through the text using an arrow key.

End key

The END key **moves the cursor** to the bottom of the screen or the end of the file on which you are working. *The function of this key could depend on the software program you are using.*

Page Up key

The Page Up key (Pg Up) **moves the cursor** up one document page or screen of information. In a word processing program, you can create documents with several pages each consisting of about 55 lines. *Depending on the software you are using*, the Page Up key will either move the cursor up a page (55 lines) or a screen (25 lines).

Page Down key

The Page Down key (Pg Dn) **moves the cursor** down one page or  screen. Like the Page Up key, Page Down functions often *depend on the software program you are using.*

Print Screen key

The Print Screen key (PrtScr) sends information you see on the screen to an attached printer, supposedly to print. It doesn't really print the *whole* file on which you are working at the time. Like it doesn't print graphics. Just text. The Print Screen key merely sends the information that you see on your screen to the printer. Be aware that it doesn't on all software programs. 

Scroll Lock key

The Scroll Lock key locks the cursor at its current position on the screen. When you press this key, the Scroll Lock LED (light) turns on. When you use the cursor movement keys, the text on the screen moves in the direction of that key. Scroll Lock can only be . used if the software has this capability. 

Pause / Break key

When you use the Pause / Break key in conjunction with the Ctrl key, you stop a program operation and "freeze" the screen until any other key is pressed. Pause / Break can only be used if the software program you are using has this capability.

Numeric Keypad

The group of keys located on the far right of the keyboard, the numeric keypad, has a dual purpose that depends on the **Num Lock** key. The Num Lock key *toggles on and off* to indicate whether you have access to the numbers or cursor control keys on the numeric keypad. *The Num Lock LED* indicates whether the Num Lock key is ON or OFF. When Num Lock is ON, you have access to the numerical operations on the keypad. When **Num Lock is OFF**, the keypad is used to control the screen cursor. 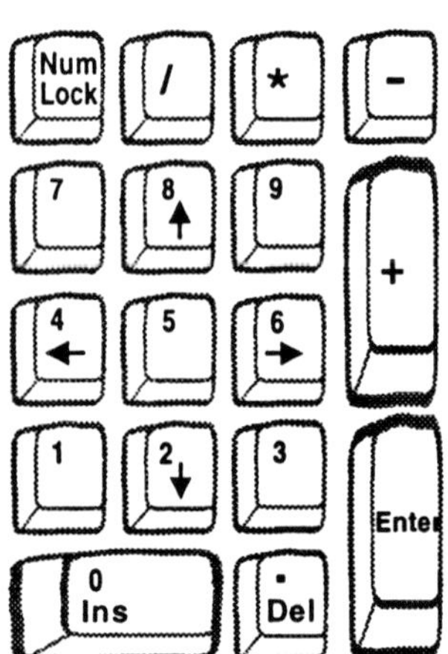

The keypad turns into a calculator when the **Num Lock key is ON**. This is helpful when you are entering a lot of numbers. The mathematical functions include *addition* (**+**), *subtraction* (**-**), *multiplication* (*****), and *division* (**/**).

When the ***Num Lock key is OFF***, you have access to the cursor control keys and the keypad acts like the keys on the Cursor Control Keypad. You will find that the following keys on the Numeric Keypad function the same way as the corresponding keys on the Cursor Control Keypad: Arrow keys, Home, Page Up (PgUp), End, Page Down (PgDn), Insert (Ins), Delete (Del).

You can also find an ENTER key on this keypad that works just like the Enter key on the main area of the keyboard.

Most folks just leave the *Num Lock key ON* because the cursor control is already available through the cursor control keypad.

Keyboard Additional Note:

Where the #@*!! is the "Any" key?
The "any" key ***DOES NOT*** exist!   When the manual text or the screen text says "Press any key to continue" it means literally that. PRESS ANY KEY ON YOUR KEYBOARD. Any number, any letter, the enter key, whichever. There is no key marked "any."   BUT if it makes it any easier, write the word "any" on any key!

"Any" exceptions to the "Any" key?? Yes! The Ctrl, Alt, Shift, and the 5 in the middle of the Numeric Keypad won't work as an "Any" key. Don't know why. Who cares!

Racing Against the Keyboard

Each software program has a different speed at which it can accept the information you are typing. *So what happens if you type faster than the program can accept?* **The keyboard can remember about 16 keystrokes** over and above what has been displayed on the screen. If you *exceed* that number, your keyboard will send electrical shocks to your fingertips. **JUST KIDDING!** The keyboard will "beep" when you exceed that number. The keys that "beeped" at you won't be displayed. *Basically, the keyboard is "full."* It's the computers way of saying "Whoa! Let me catch up." You should then wait for the program to catch up.

If the keyboard continues to "beep" every time you hit a key, chances are good you *"locked-up"* the keyboard. In that event, throw away the keyboard and get a new one. **JUST KIDDING AGAIN!** You can fix this by *resetting* the computer. When you reset, you are restarting the computer while it's on.

Here's two ways to do this: **1)** You can press and hold the *Ctrl, Alt,* and *Del* keys at the same time. Then, *let go,* you know, release the keys. **2)** If that doesn't work, look for a *reset switch* on the computer. If you've got one, *push it.*

IF ALL ELSE FAILS... There are times when Ctrl-Alt-Del won't work for you in these situations, and you don't have a reset button to push. **Now What?** You'll have to turn the computer **OFF**, then turn the computer back **ON** again.

REMEMBER... Resetting or turning OFF the computer takes you back to square one, the "C" prompt, which means anything you didn't save is lost. Keep that in mind!

Repeating Keys

Many keyboards have what is called an *auto-repeat* capability. This means that when you **hold down a key** it will repeat automatically. A perfect use of this function is to move through a document by holding down one of the cursor movement keys, such as the DOWN arrow key. Instead of repeatedly pressing the arrow key, you can just hold it down and scroll quickly through the text.

The Mouse: What Is It?

Not **all** computer items have technical sounding names. And you'll have to admit that "mouse" is a far cry from "adapter board" and "micropro-cessor." The computer world's version of the mouse does everything it can to make your life with your computer a bit easier.

Like the keyboard, the mouse is a way that you can communicate with your computer to tell it what to do. What makes it easy is that it gives you the ability to just point to a command rather than use the keyboard to type in the command.

With its little body *(fits in your hand)* and long, tail-like cable, ***it resembles a mouse.*** However, this mouse won't nibble on cheese or even move unless you move it. The mouse tail (cable) attaches to the back of your computer and enables communication between the mouse and the main system.

Initially the mouse was used mainly by artists, architects, and designers because of the *flexibility* it offered. However, since more software programs use the mouse, its use in homes, schools, and offices has increased.

How Does It Work?

The mouse is not instantly useful. The mouse only works **IF** you have the *software to support it.* As you slide the mouse around on your on your desktop, the *"mouse cursor"* or *"pointer"* moves around on the screen in the same manner. You can then move the cursor and point to a specific function you want completed instead of typing the command through the keyboard.

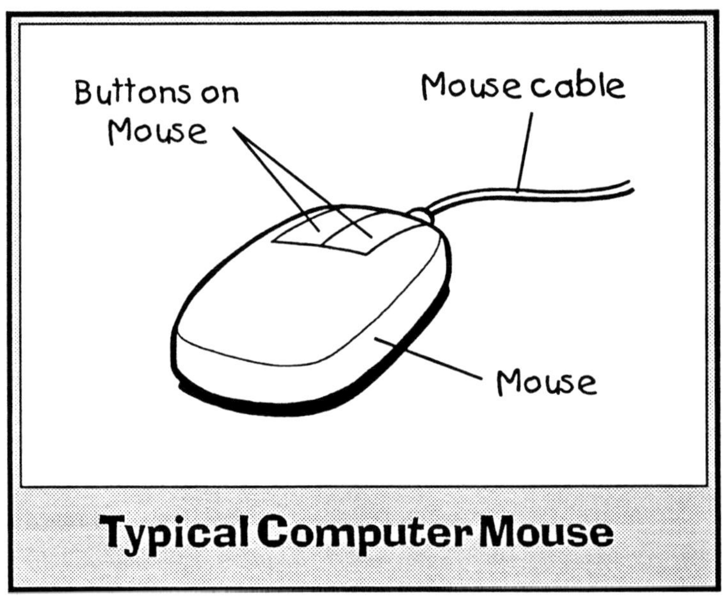

Typical Computer Mouse

The mouse has **buttons** on it that are used for *executing the commands.* They work similar to the function of the ENTER key on a keyboard. The button commands vary from program to program. The ease of use is what makes the mouse so popular.

Mouse Talk

Here are a few terms that describe *mouse action*:

Point

The small arrow that appears on your screen is the *"mouse cursor"* or *"pointer."* Moving the mouse around on your desktop will move the "pointer" on the screen in a similar manner. When you stop the pointer at a *specific* location (usually a graphic looking thing) you are "pointing." You ARE NOT breaking any politeness rules here. Pointing is encouraged.

Click

The press of a mouse button is a "click." A "click" means push the button down once and release it. When you point to a specific function and "click," you are usually activating a function to be used soon. This function may vary from program to program.

Double-click   (click-click)

O.K. You know what a click is. Pressing a mouse button twice quickly, is a "double-click." When you point to a specific function and "double-click," you are usually telling the computer "do-it," start this function. This function may also vary from program to program.

Sometimes you *double-click* the 'ol mouse and it doesn't do anything. You probably didn't do it fast enough. You gotta "click-click" as fast as you can. Software, like Windows, lets you make adjustments to clicking. *Read your manual.*

Drag

Point, press AND **hold** the mouse button down, then move your mouse around, you're not doing the "Hokey-Pokey", you are **dragging.** In effect, you are **grabbing** something and **moving it around the screen.** When you *release* the button, you are letting go of that something.

When using a mouse, you usually click and double-click on small graphical items called *"icons."* Icons are graphical *(picture)* representations of commands or software programs.

For example, if you wanted to start the WordPerfect software program, you would *point* to the icon that represents WordPerfect and *double-click* the mouse button. You will encounter icons in most software that supports the mouse.

What Did You Learn?

You now know the basics of using the *two most important ways* of interacting with your computer: the **keyboard** *and the* **mouse.** *Each key* on the keyboard has a particular name and purpose. You may have seen many of these keys before on a standard typewriter. The other keys, such as the **Function keys,** perform functions unique to the computer world and the software that you are using.

The mouse is a computer tool increasing in popularity. Designed to make communicating with computers easier, the mouse allows you to interact with graphical elements on your screen. One popular software program that supports the mouse is Microsoft Windows.

Chapter 7

The Proof Is
In The Print

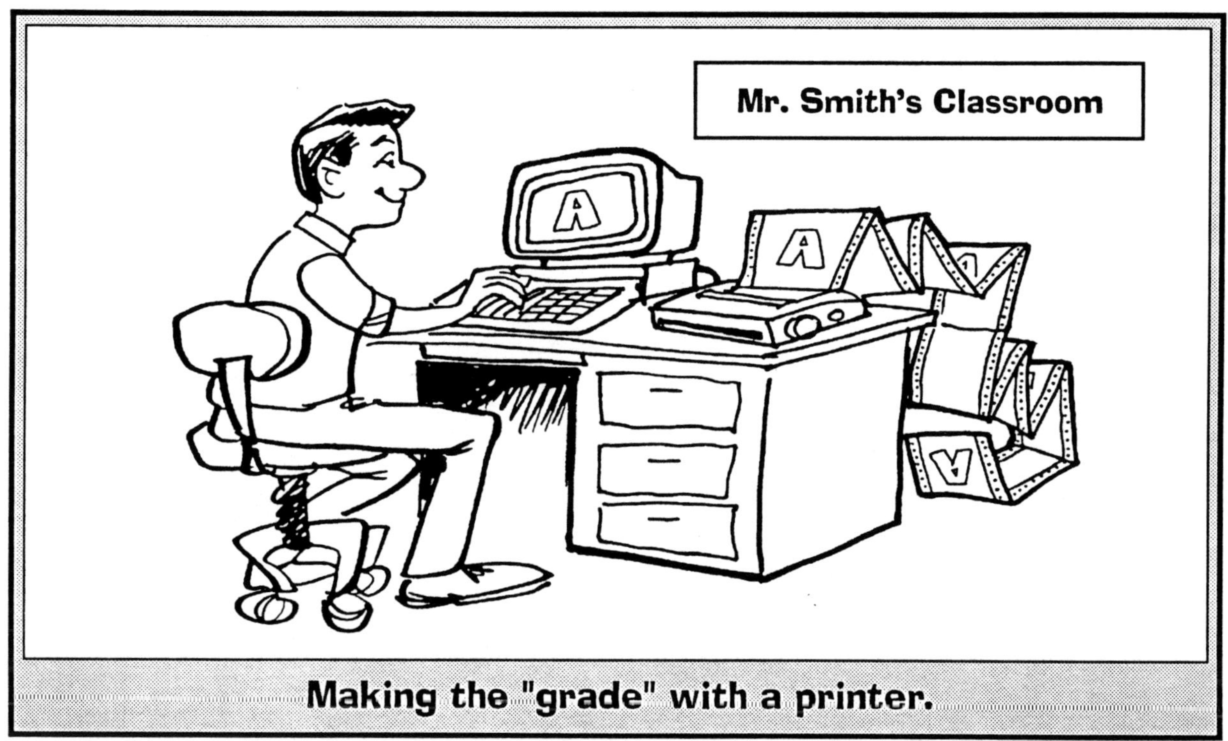

Making the "grade" with a printer.

Write a letter. Make a customer mailing list. Design a company news-letter. While everything you do on your computer can be seen on the monitor screen, you can't carry your monitor around to show people what you've done. *Without a printer*, that's what you'd have to do. A printer is not necessary to use your computer, but that's the same as saying you don't need to speak to express what you're thinking. ***The printer is the main form of expression for the computer.***

What's the point of creating letters and other documents on your computer if you can't get printed copies of them? If a computer is to be truly useful, you need a way to print the information that the computer processes.

There are many different types of printers that vary in speed, print quality and cost. When buying a printer, you will undoubtedly find that there are *trade-offs* among speed, print quality and cost. In addition, there are also differences in printer sizes and maintenance.

We're going to cover three types of popularly used printers: **dot matrix, laser,** and **ink jet.** Read on.

Dot Matrix Printers

Dot matrix printers are the *cheapest* (dollar wise) and most commonly used printers in business and in the home. They're called dot matrix because the print head uses a number of *pins* to make rows and columns (matrix) of dots to form a character. The more pins the print head contains, the better the print quality. A few features, such as continuous feed paper, give them an advantage over the more expensive printers.

The Technology

As discussed, the dot matrix printers use a series of dots to form characters. Like a typewriter, the dot matrix printer uses a ribbon that has ink on it. The characters are formed by a number of pins pushed against the ink ribbon onto the paper. These pins create the dots that form each character.

You can get either a 9-pin or 24-pin printer. The 24-pin printer will print at a higher quality because it has more pins positioned closer together. In contrast, the 9-pin printer must print characters twice to get a quality even close to the 24-pin printer. Obviously, this makes for slower printer speeds. However, the advantage of a 9-pin printer is its low cost.

Maintenance

Dot matrix printers require *little* maintenance. You will find this to be an advantage over ink jet and laser printers. Typically, you will only have to replace the dot matrix printer's typewriter-style ink ribbon periodically. These ribbons are inexpensive (about the same price as typewriter ribbons) and are easy to install.

Variety in Speed and Quality

One advantage of the dot matrix printer is that it can give you a variety of *speeds* and *quality*. These different qualities are called "draft" and "letter" quality. **Draft quality** is typically lighter and the dots that form the characters can be seen. **Letter quality** is the best quality you can get from a dot matrix printer. You can use draft quality to print some thing quickly that *does not* require a nice finished look. Then later, you can print the same document in letter quality when the final version is needed. The *speed* of a dot matrix printer slows down as the quality increases. The brochure you get with your printer should tell you the printer speed, which is measured in **pages per minute** (ppm) or **characters per second** (cps).

Paper Used

Dot matrix printers can use single sheets of paper or continuous feed paper. The great thing about continuous feed paper is its convenience. *Individual sheets of paper are connected together end to end.* Holes run down the side of the paper. Pins inside the printer hook through these paper holes to pull the roll of paper through. That means you don't have to keep feeding in single sheets of paper. You can get all kinds of paper products in a continuous feed format. *Examples:* letterhead, envelopes, checks, labels, paper of different sizes and much more.

Column Width

You will hear that a dot matrix printer is either an **80-column** or **132-column** printer. *The 80-column printer* prints pages on standard notebook-sized pieces of paper. *The 132-column printer* can print on the wider sheets of paper (132 columns) that are used for accounting and design applications. The 132-column printer can use both wide paper as well as standard notebook size paper.

Laser Printers

A Laser printer *delivers best quality, high-resolution printer output, quietly and efficiently,* giving you finished standard cut paper pages like a copy machine would. Matter of fact, they work *similar* to how a copy machine works. They're the best and if you want the best you're gonna have to pay. However, if **top print quality** and **flexibility** are important to you, then go laser.

When laser printers first came out, they were typically found in publishing and design companies, where the laser printer price was justified by its superior quality. As laser printer prices started to decrease, it's popularity increased. *Isn't that the way it always works?* Companies are doing more with their computers and print quality is becoming more important. Although you can now find a laser printer almost anywhere, they are still primarily used with desktop publishing and graphics software.

The Technology and Quality

The laser printer, *looking like a small copy machine,* actually works in a similar way. The laser printer transfers a fine black powder called *toner* to the paper. Inside the laser printer there is a roller, that when magnetized, attracts the toner. Using a little laser, the printer magnetizes this roller at specific locations. These locations match the page to be printed.

The roller then passes over the paper, transferring the toner. The toner is then heated, causing it to attach itself permanently to the paper.

Like the dot matrix printer, each character generated by the laser printer is created by dots. *But now they are created by hundreds of dots.* The laser printer dots are a lot smaller and closer together which produces a better quality character. The quality of a laser printer is usually noted by the **dots per inch** (DPI) value. *A 300 DPI* printer quality is fairly standard among laser printers. Higher quality laser printers can print as many as *600* and *1200* dots per inch.

Maintenance

A laser printer is maintained and operated **much like a copy machine** that must go through routine check ups. It also requires *toner cartridges,* which are full of dry ink, that must be replaced periodically. Toner cartridges can be expensive *(about $75-$100 each).* Laser printers are harder to maintain than dot matrix printers since their ink cartridges must be replaced periodically.

Paper Used

Unlike dot matrix printers, laser printers use **single sheets** of paper, just as a copy machine would. A typical laser printer has a sheet feeder that will hold several hundred sheets of paper. It is the fastest and quietest printer, able to print between 6 and 20 **pages per minute** (ppm). Like some copiers, it is limited to *standard* (8.5x11) and *legal* (8.5x14) size sheets. *Special* laser printer paper is available.

Ink-Jet Printers

Ink-jet printers have not been around as long as dot matrix and laser printers. They were introduced at the time when laser printer prices made such high quality printers unreachable for budget conscious computer users. In terms of price and ability, *the ink jet printer falls between the dot matrix and laser printer.* It offers *near quality of the laser printer* at less than half the price.

The Technology and Quality

The ink jet printer creates its characters by **shooting a fine jet of ink through holes in a matrix** (a pattern of rows and columns) onto the paper. The ink is taken from a small cartridge of ink that *you can buy in different colors.* The jet spray does not apply itself as accurately as a laser printer. You sometimes see a few stray "dots" outside of the characters on the paper. However, despite these few imperfections, in cluding occasional jet clogging, a good ink jet printer can produce results that are comparable to a laser.

Maintenance

As with price and quality, ink-jet printers are also in between dot matrix and laser printers when it comes to maintenance. The small cartridges of ink that the ink-jet printers use must be replaced about *every 1000 pages* or so. These ink cartridges cost $15 to $20. Most ink-jet printers use black ink, *although you can buy the ink in different colors.*

Paper Used

Like laser printers, ink-jet printers **cannot** use continuous feed paper. It uses standard-sized cut paper. Some ink-jet owners prefer to use the clay coated paper *("special" coated paper)* that is also available for the laser.

What Did You Learn?

The proof is in the print. The printer is the machine that expresses or shows the work done on the computer by putting it on paper. There are several types of printers: **dot matrix, laser,** and **ink jet**, to name a few. These printers differ in **price, print quality, speed,** and **maintenance.**

When shopping around for a printer, it is wise to evaluate your print quality needs and fit them to your budget. In general, *laser printers* serve the needs of users who demand high quality. *Ink-jet printers* serve those who want good quality at a good price. And *dot matrix printers* serve those who value durability and low price over speed and quality.

Chapter 8

Where It All Happens

When you start your car, things happen. Fans start spinning, belts start turning, and fuel starts exploding. *Get the picture?* All you really had to do was turn the key. Underneath your car's hood, a whole little world is put into motion when you start the car. *And the same can be said of a computer.*

Computers don't have hoods like cars, but they do have a central place where all of the work is done. *Generally speaking,* this main part of the computer is called the **Central Processing Unit** *(CPU),* that's the large box on which monitors usually sits. *Strictly speaking,* the microprocessor chip is called the **CPU**. However, CPU has become sort of a generic reference to the PC as a whole, referring to the "box" that contains all the other "stuff" that makes the computer do it's magic. When you start your computer, a number of components begin their work. **The CPU,** like the engine of your car, **is where all the action takes place.**

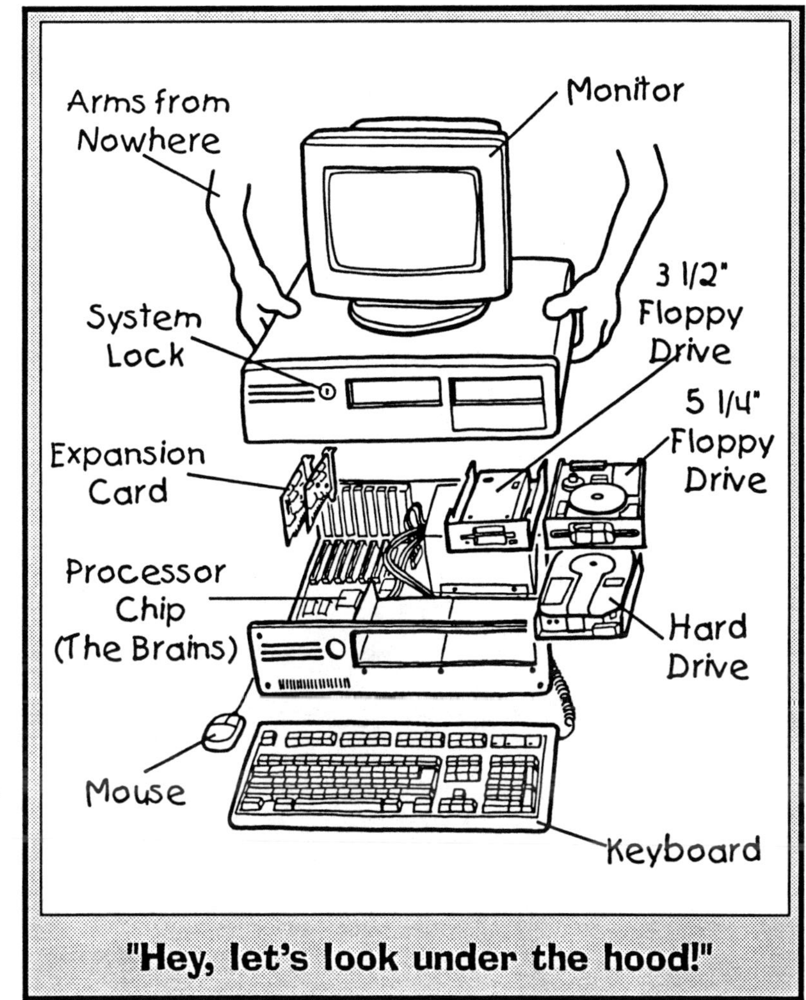

"Hey, let's look under the hood!"

In this chapter we take you on a tour of this important part of the computer. We'll look at the ***front, back,*** and ***inside*** of a standard desktop computer. Tower computers and portable computers (laptop and notebook) look physically different than the desktop computer. But all computers have the same basic components.

What's Up Front?

NOT just another pretty face! The following are brief descriptions of the some of the items found on the face, or front of a typical computer. *Some of these items are not necessarily on the front of a computer.* Position varies depending on the manufacturer.

The Front. Not just another pretty face!

LEDs

Light Emitting Diodes or Activity Indicators show you when a specific part of the computer is in use. These little *"lights"* are found on *display panels* for keyboards as well as on *hard drives* and *floppy drives*. They usually give off a red or green glow (light) but have been known to appear in other colors.

Floppy Drives

Floppy drives are probably the most noticeable items on the front of a computer. You insert floppy diskettes into the openings you see on the drives. Once inserted, the computer can read, change, delete or add information to the floppy diskette. Floppy drives are usually one of two sizes - one for **5.25"** diskettes and one for **3.5"** diskettes. Each drive has its own LED activity indicator that lights up when the drive is in use.

Floppy Drive Latch (5.25" Floppy Drive)

The floppy drive latch can be considered the **drive door.** When you insert a floppy disk into the drive, *you must close the drive door* so that the drive knows there's a disk inside. These latches may come in different shapes.

Eject Button (3.5" Floppy Drive)

On the 3.5" floppy drive, the diskette *"pops"* in and is *ejected* with an *eject button* located on the front of the drive.

Hard Drives

Usually the hard drive sits directly underneath a floppy drive on the front of a computer. The *only indication* you may find that a hard drive exists in a system is its *LED* activity indicator on the front panel of the system itself. The hard drive is a non-removable storage location for information. *More details in chapter 9.*

System Lock

Some computers come with a sort of a *computer-keyboard chastity belt.* A keyhole with a key that locks up the keyboard. This "system lock" or key lock is supposed to be some kind of security thing. When locked, the keyboard doesn't send a thing to the CPU. Prevents unauthorized use of your computer. You get the key when you buy your computer. Lose the keys *before* you accidently lock yourself out of your own computer.

Reset Button

The reset button is used to *restart* the computer. It is similar to turning the electrical power off and then on again, but not as drastic. It basically interrupts the power to the main computer chip which causes it to re-start. It is normally used when your system gets stuck (freezes-up) and your computer won't accept information from the keyboard.

What's In The Back?

*We're gonna talk **behind** the computer's back.* The following are brief descriptions on what you'll find on the *back of a typical computer.* The back of the computer, like most electrical appliances, is where all the plugs and cables are located.

System On/Off Switch

The power switch or **ON/OFF** button turns the computer on and off. This switch can sometimes be located on the front or side of the system, depending on the manufacturer.

System Power Cord

This socket is where the **main power cord** plugs into the computer. In turn, the main power cord, which is a standard AC power cord, *plugs into a standard wall outlet.* It is through this power connector that all system parts are powered.

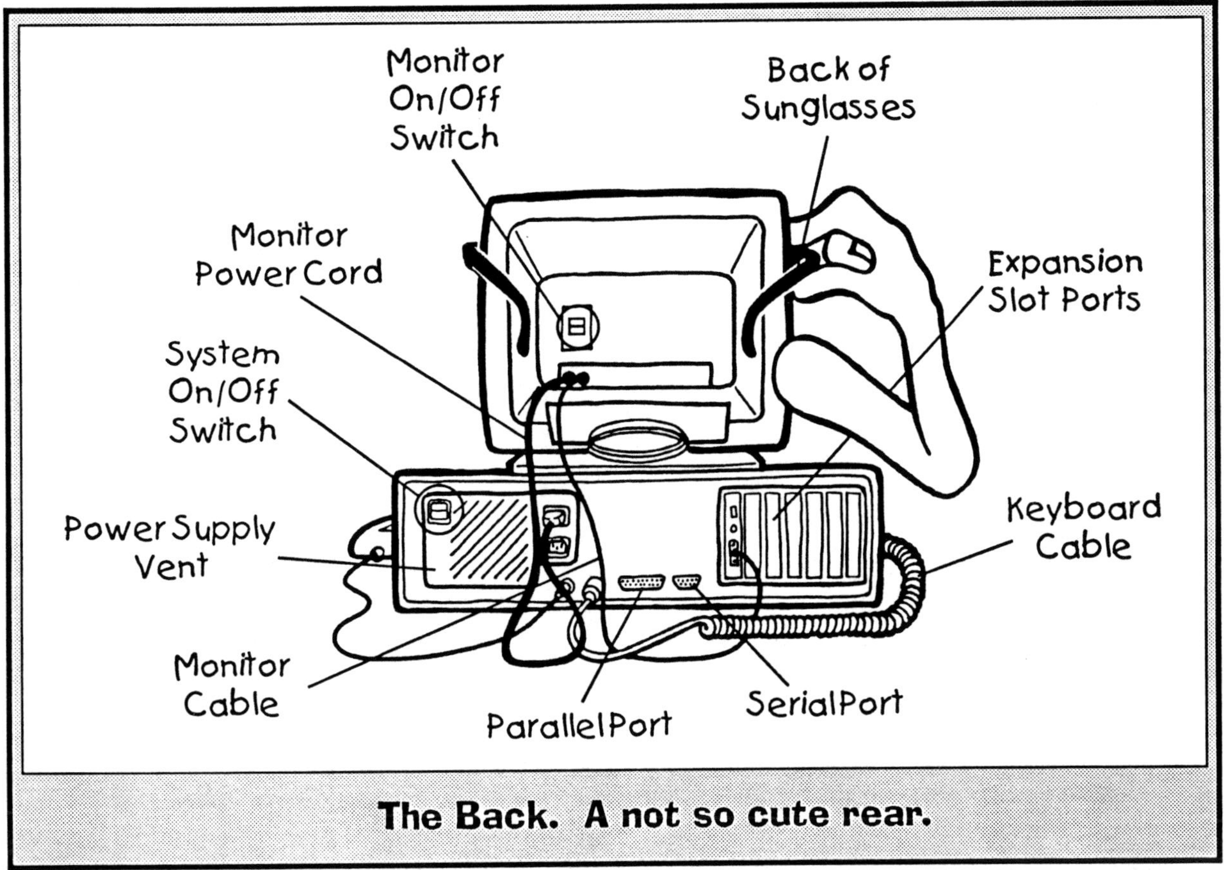

The Back. A not so cute rear.

Monitor On/Off Switch

This power switch or **ON/OFF** button turns the **monitor**...YES, on and off. Remember to turn this switch ON when you turn on the computer. You won't see anything on the screen if the monitor is not turned on. *A common mistake is to forget to turn on the monitor.* Really. Then you'll call someone asking them for help and they'll ask you "Did you turn the monitor power switch on?" and you'll say..."OOPS!"

Monitor Power Cord

The **monitor power cord** provides *electrical power to the monitor.* Some times this cord plugs directly into the back of the computer. The computer must have an appropriate socket in the back to accept the monitor power cord directly. Otherwise, a standard wall outlet would be the other place to plug into.

Monitor Cable

Besides power, the monitor needs a way to **communicate** with the main system. It's through the *monitor cable* that the monitor receives information from the computer (CPU). This cable plugs directly into the *video adapter board.* The video adapter board actually sits inside the computer with the connector part sticking out the back side of the computer. It's called a port.

Keyboard Cable and Port

The keyboard cable and port are the means by which the *keyboard and computer (CPU)* **exchange information.** That's right, this is a very important connection and you should always make sure that this cable is well secured in its socket.

Serial Port

The serial port is a connector through which the computer (CPU) **sends and receives information to any number of serial devices.** A serial device send or receives information over one wire. Serial ports are also called RS-232 (Recommended Standard 232) ports or COM (Communications) ports. No, I don't know who comes up with these names.

Most computers come with *at least one* serial port and serial ports can be added to your system. You gotta buy 'em. *The most common items plugged into a serial port?* A serial mouse, serial printers, modems, or other serial devices.

Parallel Port

The parallel port is a connector through which the computer (CPU) **sends and receives information to a parallel device.** A parallel device sends or receives information over eight wires at a time, and as such, is much faster than a serial port. *Printers are the most common item plugged into a parallel port.*

Expansion Slot Ports

These are *"holes"* in the back of the computer that allow external access to the **expansion boards** that you may want to install in the computer. These holes have *covers* on them until you install an expansion board. We will discuss the expansion boards later.

Power Supply Vent

This vent *allows heat to escape* from inside the system. With 3 or 4 electrically powered devices running inside the computer at the same time, the inside has a tendency to get hot. A fan, just inside the power supply, helps to keep the system cool.

What's Inside That Metal Box?

The *operation, calculations and processing* the computer makes does not happen magically. A number of devices inside the computer work together to process everything the computer does. All of these processing devices are located inside the "CPU." the metal box usually underneath your monitor. (Look at the picture at the start of this chapter.)

In this section, we open up the *"box"* and take a look inside. You may find it less confusing than you think. You'll mostly see *green circuit boards, computer chips, cables and storage drives.* That's about it. And they are all laid out and connected logically.

You should not try to open up your CPU unless you're an experienced user and you understand how everything works. In other words, **don't try this at home** (or in the office). If you do attempt this, make sure you **UNPLUG the power** supply to the system. *O.K.?*

So... What's inside?

The Motherboard

Because the motherboard is such an important part of the computer, we are going to go into a few more details about it. We'll discuss the different parts of the motherboard so you can see how they all work together.

If you were to open the box (CPU), and look down to the bottom of the system unit, you'd see one big, usually green, circuit board that houses the **microprocessor chip** (the "brains"), the computer's **memory** (RAM), **expansion slots** (receptacles that accept additional expansion boards), and *other stuff* that supports the general performance of the computer. This board, most commonly called the **Motherboard,** also known as the system board, is the largest and most important board in the computer. Every part of a computer, both inside and out, is somehow connected to the motherboard.

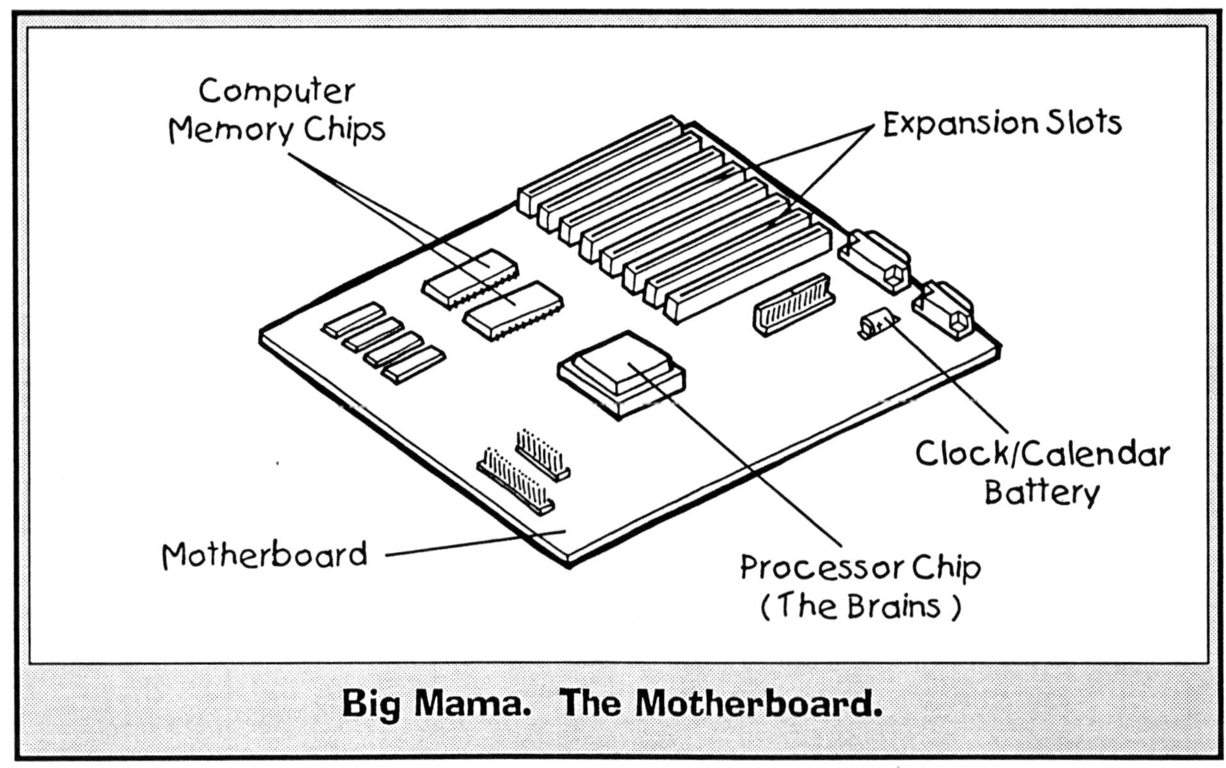

Big Mama. The Motherboard.

Microprocessor Chip ("The Brains")

Found on the motherboard, the **microprocessor chip** is a computer chip that has been designed for the specific purpose of *processing information.* It performs all of the required calculations for the computer system. It is also responsible for coordinating communication between the various parts of the computer system. Once it does its computations, it sends the results to the appropriate device. Kind of amazing that this chip, *usually no bigger than a dime,* can perform these calculations in such a short period of time.

There are several types of microprocessor chips available along with different names for them. **Central processing unit (CPU)** and **processor** are names used to refer to the chip along with numbers like the ***8088, 80286, 80386, 80486*** and probably real soon, the *80586* or something more powerful than the 80486 with a fancy number assigned to it.

These days, when computer users ask each other what type of PC they have, they typically say: *"Is it a 286, or a 386, or a 486?"* The "80" in front of the number is dropped.

Generally speaking, the bigger the number, the faster and more powerful the computer. *Oh yeah,* the bigger the number, the higher the price tag.

The letters SX and DX sometimes follow the processor chip number, as in the *"386**SX**"* or *"386**DX**". The difference?* The SX type chip can be compared to a *4 cylinder engine* in a car, where the DX chip is an *8 cylinder* version of the same car. The car with the 4 cylinder (SX) engine will get you to where you're going **but not as fast** as the car with the 8 cylinder (DX) engine. The SX offers the full performance of the chip, but only half the power. *The benefit?* **It'll get the job done,** not as fast, but it won't cost as much $$$.

Microprocessor Speed (How Fast Can It Think?)

Similar to a heartbeat, information moves through the processor chip at regular intervals. These intervals, called the *"clock speed"*, are measured in **megahertz** (MHz), where mega means *"million"* and hertz means your computer's in pain, *ha-ha, just kidding,* hertz means *"cycles per second."* So a *16MHz processor* processes information at a rate of *16 million cycles per second.*

Clock speeds can range from 4.77MHz to 66MHz. In order to understand this range of clock speeds, you can think of it as traveling by car or by jet. Keep in mind that some cars are faster than other cars. Same with jets. O.K.?

If you were traveling from California to New York by *Volkswagen,* you could think of it as traveling at about 4.77MHz clock speed. Now, if you travel the same distance by *Jet,* you could equate that to a 66MHz clock speed. You'll eventually get there but one will get you there faster than the other.

The big question is, would you rather go by Volkswagen or a jet? If you do fairly simple activities, like word process ing, then a slower system (microprocessor) will do. But if your work involves many calculations or extensive graphics works, then you might be better off buying *a first class plane ticket* - a fast microprocessor.

Math Coprocessor

The math coprocessor is an *optional* computer chip that can be put on the motherboard. It works with the standard processor to *process numerical information*. A standard processor can process numerical information by itself, the coprocessor just speeds it up. The math coprocessor chip is usually **NOT** necessary unless you plan to do a lot of calculations.

Computer Chips

The *black rectangular things* that you see on the motherboard and the expansion boards are called *computer chips*. If you pulled a computer chip from the circuit board, you would find that it has a number of legs, similar to an insect. These legs connect the chip to the circuit board.

Computer chips are *very important* to a computer. Each chip is designed for a specific function. Some chips, called *memory chips*, hold data in temporary storage. Other chips, like the *microprocessor* and *math coprocessor chips*, do all the intensive calculations that computers are known for. The function of a circuit board is determined by the type of chips installed on it.

Memory Chips

Memory chips are computer chips that **store information** on either a *temporary* or *permanent* basis. This type of storage is separate from storage in a storage drive (i.e., hard drive). You will usually have *two types of memory chips* on your motherboard: **RAM** and **ROM.**

RAM, which is short for *"Random Access Memory"*, stores information on a *temporary* basis. ROM, *"Read Only Memory"*, stores information on a *permanent* basis.

RAM, or random access memory, is a **temporary storage place** for the information you are using most often. The main processor can access the information in RAM *faster* than information on a storage drive. *So once you start a program,* the system usually puts that program into RAM, where it can access it freely and quickly.

However, the *drawback* to RAM is that it will only store information as long as power to the computer is *on*. The information in RAM **disappears** when the computer turns *off*. **That's why it's important to *"save"* your work to a storage drive before switching off the computer.**

ROM, or *read only memory*, stores valuable information about the system. *This information can be read, but not changed.* Each time you switch on the computer, the system looks at the ROM chip for important instructions on starting up the system.

The Expansion Boards

Expansion Boards, Option Boards, Adapter Boards... we're talking about the smaller green circuit boards that are installed standing up into the motherboard in locations called *expansion slots*. In some cases the word "card" is used to replace the word "board" as in expansion card. They all refer to the same thing. We'll call them expansion boards, O.K.?

Once connected to the motherboard, the expansion board begins to manage the **communication between** the motherboard and the device controlled by the expansion board. For example, the video expansion board allows communication between the monitor and the motherboard.

Expansion Slots

Expansion slots allow you to add optional "things" (devices) to your computer by inserting expansion boards. *Each expansion slot is connected directly to the motherboard,* allowing the computer's microprocessor (CPU) to communicate with the device you add.

The *number* of expansion slots in a computer will vary depending on the computer. Typically, a computer will have a total of six or eight expansion slots. If you are looking to grow with your system, the number of expansion slots could be a buying factor.

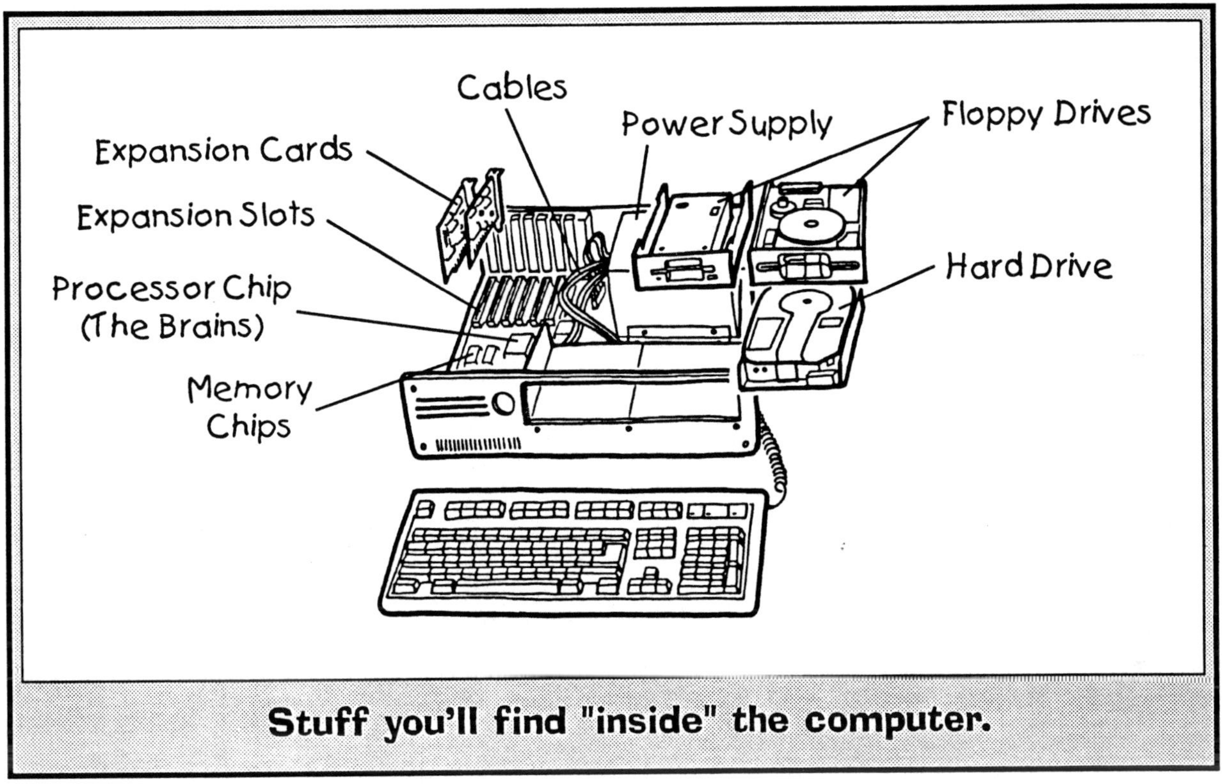

Stuff you'll find "inside" the computer.

Power Supply

The power supply is probably the biggest system component inside the computer (box). It's a *big metal box with wires coming out of it* (imagine an octopus). This is where the system's **electricity is generated.** The electrical cord is plugged into it through the back of the computer. Then, the power supply distributes the electricity through cables to all the necessary parts of the computer, such as the system board, floppy and hard drives.

Storage Drives

Next to the power supply, the *storage drives* (floppy drives and hard drives) are the biggest system components inside the computer. On the front of the computer we saw the *"front"* of these storage drives. And now, while inside the system, we get to see the rest of these drives.

These storage drives have power cables that connect with the power cables that come out of the "Octopus", the power supply. In addition, these drives usually have cables that connect them to an expansion board in an expansion slot. The expansion slot is connected to the motherboard and now everything is communicating. You know, the foot bone's connected to the ankle bone and the ankle bone's connected... etc.

Cables

As you are probably aware of by now, everything inside the computer needs some way to talk to the other parts of the computer. *Most of this communication occurs through cables.* The cables inside the system are either **ribbon cables** (for communication) or **power supply cables** (for electricity).

Ribbon Cables

The wide, flat, multi-wire cables. These cables enable *communication between various parts of the system.* Mostly the parts that have circuit boards (those green boards) on them or *they are* circuit boards. An example would be the ribbon cable that connects the hard drive to the motherboard

Power Supply Cables

The main parts of the computer, such as storage drives and the motherboard, all need to receive electrical input to operate. The *power supply cables provide this power.*

CMOS Battery (clock/calendar battery)

Every computer has a **small battery,** much like an "AA" battery or a wrist-watch "cell" battery. This battery is called the *CMOS* battery or the *Clock/Calendar* battery. However, *this battery does not power your system.* It merely holds important system information, such as the system configuration and the date and time, in a computer memory chip called CMOS. *(O.K., if you really want to know, CMOS stands for **C**omplementary **M**etal **O**xide **S**emiconductor. Happy?)* The battery keeps the CMOS (memory) "alive" **when the computer's switched off or unplugged.** In most cases, these batteries last several years. If your computer starts to reflect the wrong date and time or your monitor displays a message about invalid set up information during start-up, you may need to replace this battery. Let a computer retailer or an experienced user do this for you.

What Did You Learn?

In this chapter we toured the main part of you computer, the **Central Processing Unit (CPU).** Everything in your system joins together inside the CPU. More specifically, everything attaches to the motherboard, which is usually located on the *"floor"* of your system.

We also touched briefly on storage drives and memory in this chapter. There is a lot more to this chapter than just pieces of hardware that are responsible for information storage. So the next chapter is devoted entirely to the subject of memory and data storage.

Chapter 9

The Computer's Filing Cabinet: Storage Drives

O.K. We all know what filing cabinets are used for in the typical office/work environment. *Right?* You know, you type a letter, receive a memo or a bill and when you're done with it you stick it in a filing cabinet. Got the picture? O.K.

Well...The computer has its' own version of *"filing cabinets"* and they're called **STORAGE DRIVES**. Information is stored on these storage drives in the form of *program files* (software programs that you buy) and *data files* (the files *you* create using these software programs.) We'll discuss program files (*software*) in Chapter 11 and data files (the files you create) in Chapter 13.

Files. They gotta go somewhere!

In this chapter, you'll learn about the different *types* of storage. Several different types of storage exist that can be used on a computer. Some store *thousands of pages* of text. Some store quite a bit less. Others have the advantage of portability and speed. We'll also cover information on memory chip storage. So hang on and pay attention!

The Two Types of Storage

In the standard computer system there are *two ways* of storing information. __*Disk Drives*__, which include *floppy drives* and *hard drives*, store information on a permanent basis. Floppy and hard drives consist of electronically coated media platters on which data is stored. Disk drives are used to store information on a long-term basis.

__*Memory Chips*__ are much, much smaller than disk drives and usually store less information than disk drives. One type of memory chip, **RAM** *(Random Access Memory)*, can only store information on a temporary basis. However, RAM is the fastest memory around and it allows your system to complete its task efficiently. The other kind of memory chip is called **ROM** *(Read Only Memory)*. ROM permanently stores information crucial to the operation of your computer.

In this chapter we cover both **disk drives** and **memory chips**.

Disk Drives

The two main types of storage disk drives are **floppy drives** and **hard drives.** Most computer systems will contain *both types* of drives. With floppy drives, the disk is **removable**. It can be taken out of the drive. With a hard drive, the disk is **not removable**. It is a permanent part of the drive and it stays in there.

The floppy drive, since it uses removable media, called disks or diskettes, is valuable for *transporting data* between computers. The hard drive, permanently mounted inside your computer, can hold much more information than the floppy drives, so it is normally used to store software for the long term.

Floppy Disk Drives

Every computer has a least one floppy disk drive. These floppy drives use **removable** media called **diskettes**. *(Diskettes are discussed in detail in Chapter 10.)* These floppy disk drives and diskettes come in two sizes: **5 1/4 inch** and **3 1/2 inch**. The size refers to the diameter of the disk.

Compared to the hard disk, the floppy disks store much less information and access to that information is ***much slower***. *IF* you could take a peek inside the floppy drive with a diskette inserted, you would see the single diskette platter spin around about 5 times in a second. Slow, compared to the hard drive at 60 spins a second.

The benefits of a floppy drive? Well, your software application programs come on floppy diskettes so you gotta have a floppy drive or you can't use the programs, which in turn would make your computer useless. Floppy drives are also used to *transfer data* between computers, therefor it has the benefit of portability (as long as the computers are compatible and have the same type of floppy drive.)

Hard Disk Drives

Also called "fixed" disk drives because they are ***non-removable***. The hard disk drive has the advantage of *storing lots more information* than the floppy disk.

It is also ***much faster*** than the floppies. *IF* you could take a peek inside, you would see several round media platters spin around about 60 times in a second. (Give or take 1 or 2 spins.) This action allows *fast access* to your software programs and information files. Typical hard disk drives hold 20Mb (small by today's standards) to *several hundred* Mb of information. (Mb is an abbreviation for megabyte. That explanation is coming up.)

Reading & Writing to Your Disks

To **read** (look at) or **write** (record) information on your disks, the disk drives have something called ***read/write heads***. *Similar to what a needle is to a record player*, the read/write heads move in and out to access the entire disk as the disk spins. The read/write heads are attached to arms in much the same way as the needle is attached to the record player arm.

The concept behind getting the information onto these "disks" is not too different from recording messages onto your answering machines. And like retrieving messages on your answering machine, you can *retrieve* the disk's information today, tomorrow or next month, that's if you don't write over or erase the information.

The following illustration shows what the inside of a *typical hard drive* would look like *if* you could see inside.

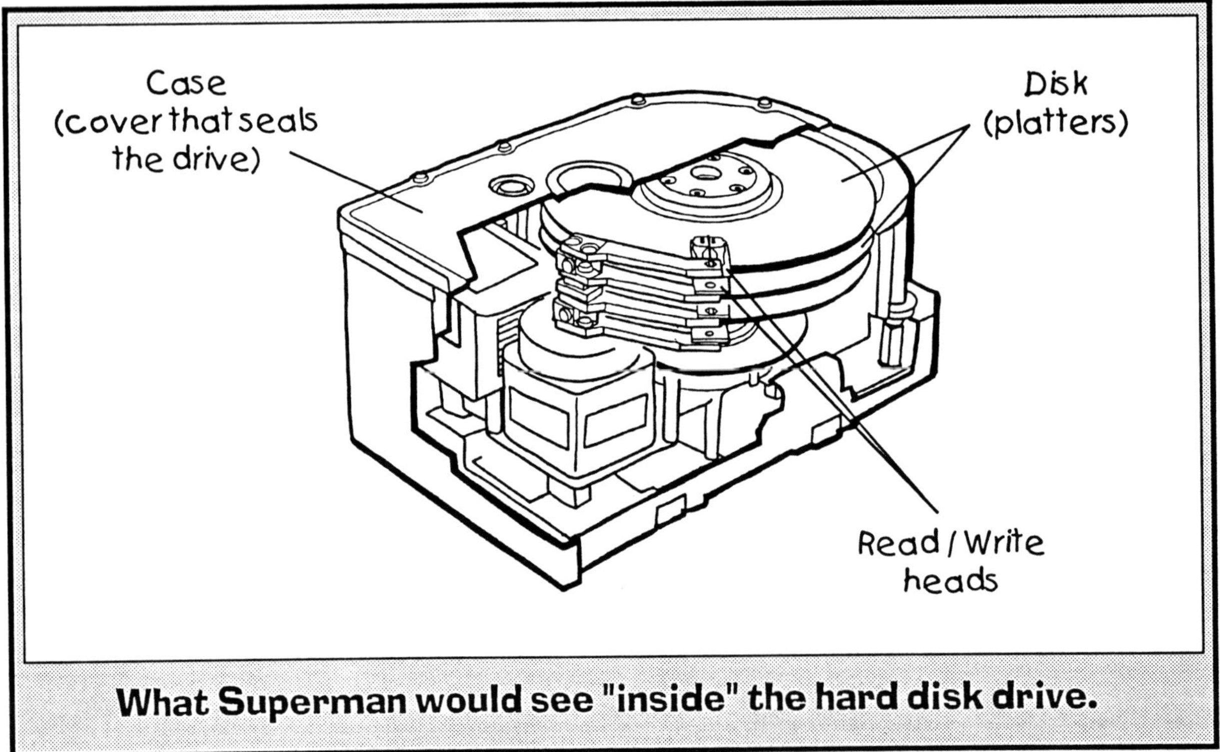

What Superman would see "inside" the hard disk drive.

How Is Storage Measured?

When *storing information* on your disk drives (hard or floppy) you are **creating files.** These files may contain a letter you typed in a word processing software program or a holiday card mailing list you created using a database software program. The software programs you use to do these things *also* create files.

As you create these *"files"*, you are taking up space on these disk drives. The amount of information that can be stored on a disk is called the *disk drive capacity.* Capacity in the computer world is measured in the form of **"bytes."** "Byte" is the term used in *computer talk* to describe file sizes.

The basic idea is a byte is the amount of space required to store a character of information.

> ***Example.*** The word **COMPUTER** takes up **8 bytes** of space on your disk. There are *8 letters* in the word COMPUTER.
> The word **IDIOT** requires **5 bytes.** There are *5 letters* in the word IDIOT. *Getting the picture?* You've taken up a total of **13 bytes** (8+5=13) of space on your disk.

How is storage measured?

Hard Disk Drives

Yeah, I know, we've already talked about hard disk drives *but it's worth touching on again.* Here's just a little more detail on an important part of the computer. So hang in there, O.K.?

The *hard disk drive* is a device that contains the storage **disk platters** (hard, *not floppy,* flat round things) and the **read/write heads** sealed in a hard metal casing. (See illustration two pages ago.) Although the hard disk has the advantage of storing a lot more information than diskettes, it is **not removable** like the diskette. It is usually *mounted securely inside the computer.*

Inside the hard disk drive there may be *several* individual "platters" with the ability to record data on both sides, along with the read/write heads located on both sides of the platters. Remember, the heads are attached to arms in much the same way as a needle is attached to a record player arm.

What Are They Used For?

Hard disk drives offer *fast and easy access* to large amounts of information *without* requiring you to insert and remove diskettes. For this reason, the hard disk drive is typically used as a ***primary storage*** place for software programs and information files. With the hard drive permanently mounted in the computer, your programs and information are readily accessible.

How Much Information Can It Hold?

Hard disk drives vary in capacities (the amount of information they hold). A typical hard disk drive can hold ***as little as 20Mb*** of information, approximately 10,000 pages of text (small by today's standards), to ***several hundred Mb*** of information. As you recall, earlier in this chapter we discussed how storage is measured and we defined Mb (megabyte).

You'd be surprised at how fast hard disk space can be used up. *Remember,* all of your software is usually stored on the hard disk. Depending on how you are using your computer, software programs can take up a lot of hard disk space.

Here's an example: a typical wordprocessing program can take up to 5Mb of hard disk space *just for the software program.* That doesn't include the space you'll use **using** the program. If you've got a 20Mb hard drive, you have just used up **25%** of the disk space available.

Here's A Tip!
The *key* to choosing the right **hard drive capacity** is to determine what storage you need today then *triple it* to incorporate future growth.

If you buy a hard drive that you outgrow, you'll be looking at the cost of a new, larger hard drive *(more dollar$.)* someone to expertly install it *(more dollar$)* and the hassle of transferring all your programs/files to the new hard drive *(you'll probably have to pay someone for that too!)* So it pays to plan ahead.

Benefits of A Hard Drive
Remember that hard disk drives are basically the computers version of the office *"filing cabinets."* Size wise, where floppy drives are like a *file folder,* limited in storage space, hard drives are like the whole *filing cabinet,* unlimited in storage, *depending on the size of your hard drive* (filing cabinet). Listed below are the benefits of a hard drive:

1) *Fast and easy access* to information without having to insert and take out diskettes as in a floppy drive.

2) *Stores large amounts* of information/data files.

3) All information, software, and data, is *stored in one place.*

4) *Permanently mounted* in the computer so you can't lose the information, as is possible with diskettes.

Other Types of Storage Drives

Floppy and hard drives are by far the most widely used storage drives. However, there are other types of drives that have more specific uses for data storage.

Tape drives are widely used for *backing up* important information on your hard drive for safety reasons. And ***optical drives*** are growing in popularity as the demand for high capacity, high-performance drives increases. Let's take a quick look at these drives.

Tape Drives

Tape media cassettes are *very similar to music tape cassettes.* If you want to hear a specific song, you have to *forward or rewind* to a specific location. This is also how tape drives work. Since tape drives move through data in sequence, the time they take to access information is often very slow. You can see that this type of storage is not practical for a primary storage drive.

Because tape media is *removable,* it is primarily used to "back up" information from your computer's hard drive. Tape cassettes provide safe storage in case something happens to the hard drive in your system. You can also use diskettes for backing up data, but tape cassettes can hold up to a *100 times more information* than diskettes.

Optical Drives

Optical media is the *latest technology for storage drives.* They are very much like music Compact Discs (CDs). The information is read and written to the media with *optical beams* rather than the standard read/write heads found on the hard and floppy disk drives.

Optical storage also allows you to store large amounts of information in a smaller space. Similar to diskettes, optical media is removable and transportable. But unlike diskettes, the optical media is hard, and it can *store much more information* than a diskette.

Optical drives are also a lot faster than floppy disk drives. If optical technology keeps improving and prices drop further, you may see this kind of drive replace the hard drive.

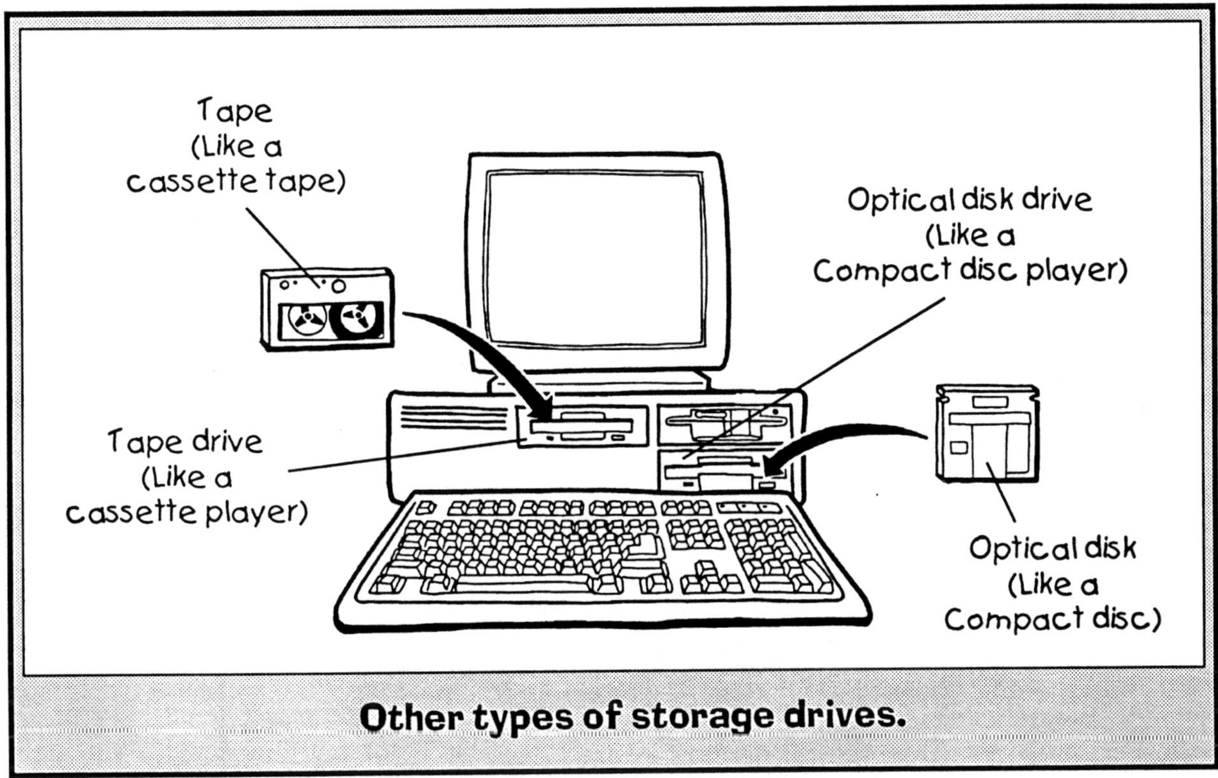

Other types of storage drives.

The ABC's Of Disk Drives

A computer system can have a combinations of storage drives. But it *(the computer)* can only work with **one storage drive at a time.** So it's important that you know how it identifies these various drives when you're looking for a specific piece of information.

Drive ID Name
Each drive has its own ID, which is represented by a letter of the alphabet. This helps you and the computer keep track of where information is stored.

The letters "A" and "B" are reserved for the floppy drives on your computer. The computer **always** has a drive "A". The floppy drive *closest to the top* of the computer is usually drive "A". *If there is a second floppy drive* it's assigned the letter "B." The ***first*** hard disk drive is always called drive "C", even if there is no floppy drive "B." After that, any additional hard drives are lettered "D," "E," "F," etc.

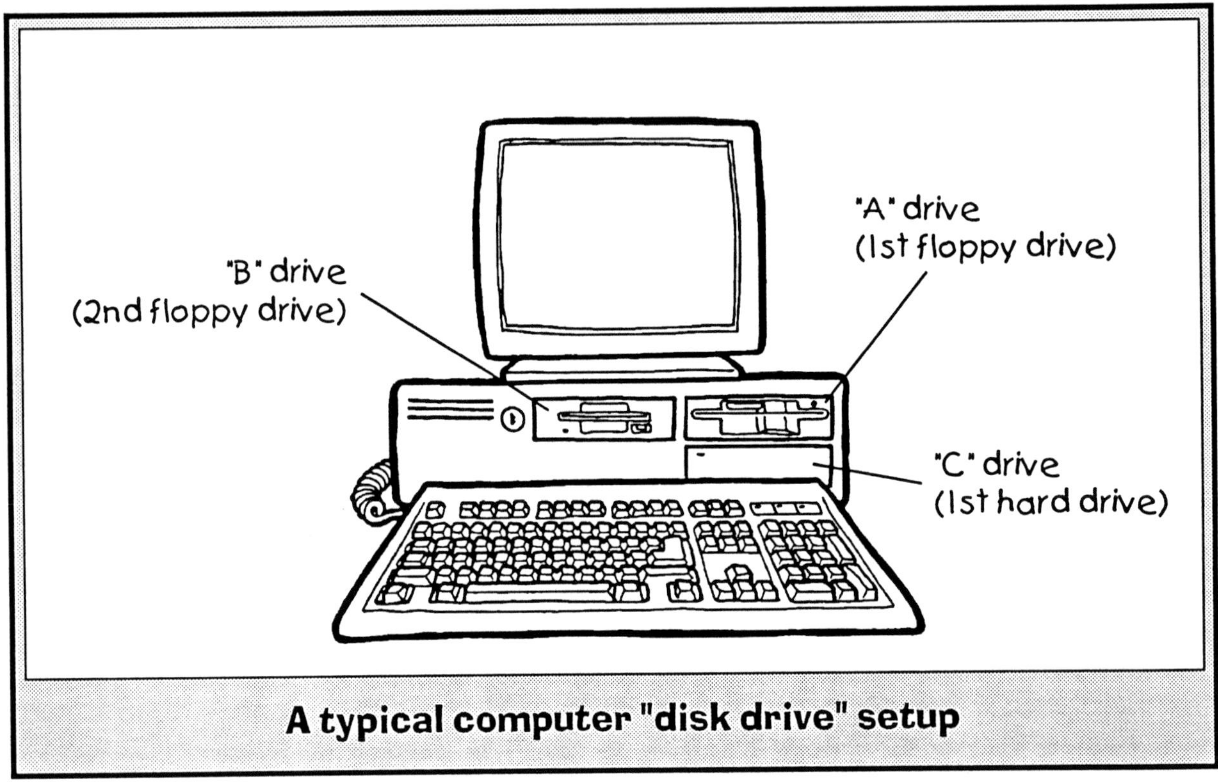

A typical computer "disk drive" setup

Changing Disk Drives

To **change** from one drive to another, for example from the "A" *(floppy)* drive to the "C" *(hard)* drive, **simply type the drive's letter**, in this case **"C"**, followed by a colon (:), then **press enter**.

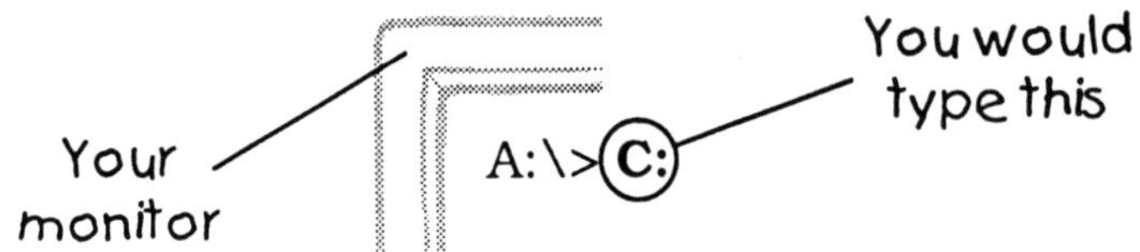

If you wanted to change from drive "C" to drive "B," you'd type:

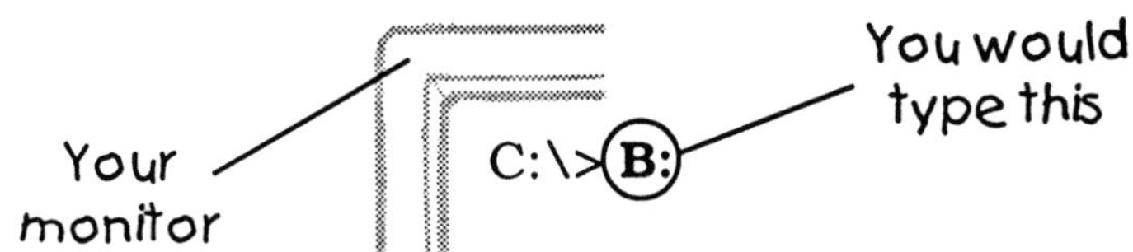

Remember... when changing disk drives with DOS, your drive letter will always be followed by a colon (:).

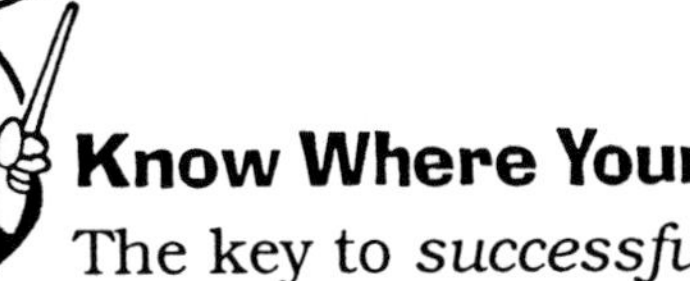

Know Where Your Stuff (Data) Is Located

The key to *successful computing* is knowing **where** you information is located. You now know that each drive is assigned an ID letter. So...

1) The first thing you need to know is the **drive** on which your information is stored.

2) The second thing is to know the **file name** you have given that piece of information.

Knowing these two facts will keep you organized. We will give you more tips on organizing your disk drives in chapter 12.

Memory Chip Storage

The computer has **another type** of storage device other than the storage drives we've already discussed. *This storage device* is in the form of a computer chip that stores information separate from storage drives. This is called a **memory chip**. *Basically,* computer chips in general are black rectangular and square things you see inside a computer that are stuck to different circuit boards. Each chip is designed for a specific function. *Therefore,* a memory chip is designed to **remember** and **store information.**

There are basically ***two types*** of memory chips:

ROM *(Rhymes with Mom)*
Read Only Memory

RAM *(Rhymes with Sam)*
Random Access Memory

What Is ROM?

ROM (Read Only Memory), stores valuable information that *only the manufacturer* (or computer expert) can change. The computer can **only read** the information. The information on this chip remains the same whether the system is ON or OFF. The ROM chip is located on the motherboard (main computer circuit board.)

ROM stores computer instructions called the *BIOS*, which stands for **Basic Input/Output System.** You may hear the two terms combined as "ROM BIOS". *ROM tells the computer what to do when the computer's power is turned on.* For example, when you start the computer, it needs to know enough to perform a self test and to load the operating system from disk. ***ROM is the memory chip that is preprogrammed*** with these needed instructions. It's sort of like having a physical exam of your body every morning and then getting the o.k. from the doctor to start your day.

What Is RAM?

RAM (Random Access Memory), is a **short term memory chip** that only works while the computer is ON. *RAM stores information that your computer needs quick access to.* When you are storing or installing your software programs, you usually put them in your hard disk drive. But when you go to use your programs, the operating system (usually DOS) reaches into your hard disk and takes a *"copy"* of the program you want to use and sticks it in RAM. The program is then "started" from RAM. So, this makes RAM a key player in the computer system.

How Is RAM Measured?

RAM is measured like storage media, **in bytes of information**. The standard RAM sizes in a computer is typically *640Kb to 2Mb*, although these days, **RAM is expandable** on some systems to 64Mb. (*Remember,* we discussed storage measurement earlier in this chapter.) You can purchase additional RAM for your system if your system has the RAM expansion capabilities.

How Is RAM Used?

The *basic concept* behind RAM is that it is used as a **temporary** holding point for only the information you need to access at that time. This allows *fast access* to the information you are currently using and leaves the other information on your storage drive.

Imagine the top of your desk as RAM and look at your filing cabinet as your hard drive. *Remember* that **RAM** *(your desk)* is only a *temporary* storage area. You have immediate access to everything on your desk. If you wanted to work with your files you would go to your **hard drive** *(filing cabinet)* and bring the files into RAM *(your desk)* to be worked on. If RAM *(your desk)* is already full, you'd have to put a few of the files you are not using back into the hard drive *(filing cabinet)* to make room for the new files you need. The smaller the RAM *(your desk)* the more often you'll return files back to the hard drive *(filing cabinet)* to make room for the new files in RAM (your desk). Turn the page and check out the illustration with *our view* of RAM.

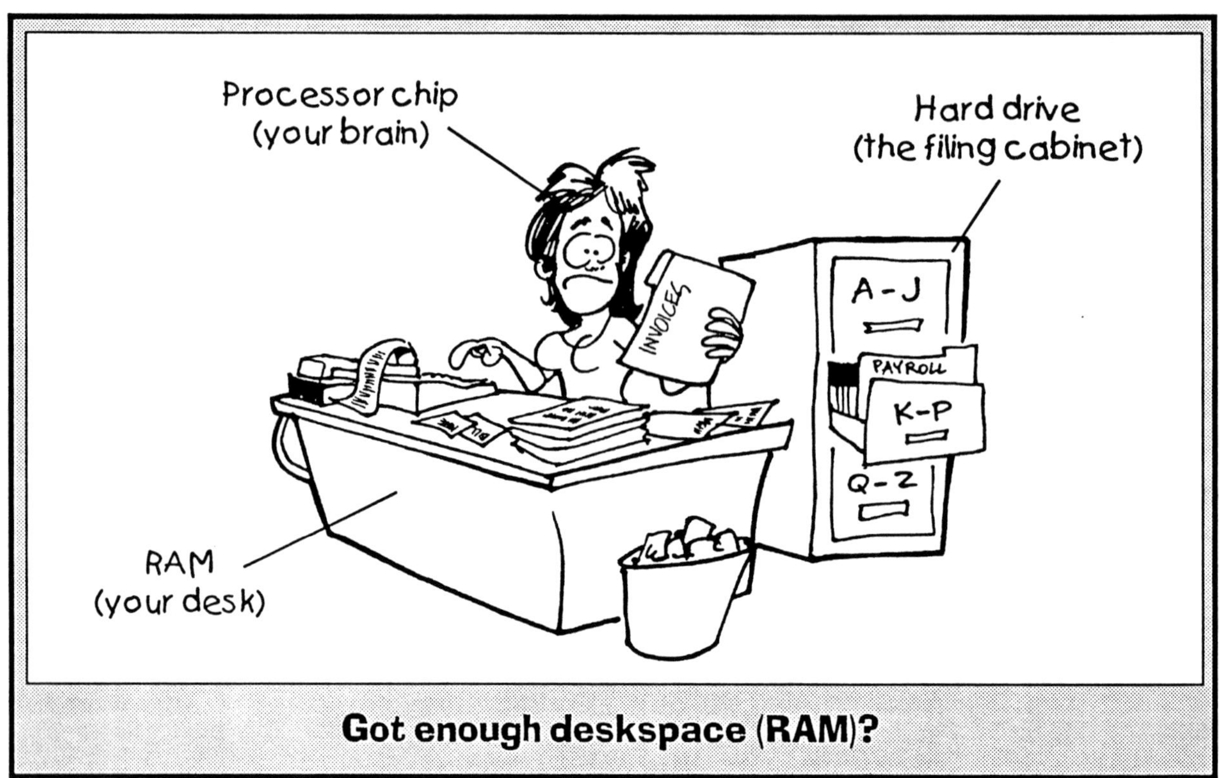

Got enough deskspace (RAM)?

Here's A Tip!
Make sure your equipment comes with enough RAM
(big enough desk) to meet the requirements of the type of
software you plan to use. RAM requirements are usually listed
on the software package.

RAM and ROM: How Do They Compare?

There are *three basic differences* between RAM and ROM. These differences
concern whether *information can be* **changed**, if the amount of *memory can be*
increased, and what's the **permanence** of the memory.

You can *change* information in RAM, but you can't in ROM. You can *add* RAM to your system, but you cannot add ROM (although you can upgrade it). And RAM holds information *temporarily* only while the computer is on, whereas the information in ROM is always there.

What Did You Learn?

One of the great things about a computer is that it can *store so much information.* It uses **storage drives** and **memory chips** for storing data. And each type of storage offers different advantages. *Disk drives*, especially hard drives, can *store thousands and thousands of pages of information.*

Memory chips offer a fast type of memory storage. RAM and ROM usually *cannot store as much information* as storage drives, but they offer the computer a very fast alternative for information retrieval. The computer relies on these memory chips to store information it will need quick access to, just as you, the computer user, rely on the storage drives and diskettes to store the information files that you will later need access to.

Chapter 10

All About Diskettes

Diskettes... *also known as floppy disks or floppies,* come in a couple of different shapes and sizes. These *things* are removable storage media that you use with your computer's floppy disk drives to **store and retrieve data**. Although the floppy disk drive *itself* is mounted permanently in the computer, the diskette media is **removable** *and* **transportable**.

Typically, these diskettes *(that's what we'll call them)* come in two sizes: **5 1/4-inch** and **3 1/2-inch**. The size refers to the diameter of the disk. (Actually, you can measure the length of a disks edge and come up with the same dimensions. *It doesn't matter which edge 'cause diskettes are square.)*

The 5 1/4-inch disk has a *thin, flexible cover* whereas the 3 1/2-inch disk has a *hard plastic cover.* By the way, these diskette covers come in all kinds of *designer colors* to match your moods when working with your computer. Now that I think about it, most diskettes come in *black.* Hmmm?

Anyway, enclosed inside these covers are **very thin, flexible** storage disk media. The diskette got the name *"floppy"* because the media disk inside is *flexible.* The area of these covers **that exposes** the media enables the floppy drives *read/write heads* to access the information on the disk. (The same concept as the read/write heads we discussed with hard disk drives in chapter 9.)

How Are They Used?

Diskettes offer removable *and therefor* transportable information. They are generally used to allow different computers to **share information** and as a way to **sell** and **distribute software programs**. Because software programs are sold on diskettes, a floppy disk drive is pretty much a requirement in your computer.

Diskettes are also used to **copy information** from your hard drive. This duplicate form, called a backup copy, ensures that your data will not be lost in case something happens to the other drives on your system.

Diskettes are to a *floppy disk drive* what **cassette** tapes are to a *cassette player.* If you're listening to a cassette tape in your car and want to continue listening to it at another location, you can. Simply remove it from your car's cassette player and insert it into another cassette player.

This concept is pretty much the same with diskettes, except that the type of diskette you use must be compatible with the floppy disk drive. We'll talk about this diskette to floppy disk drive compatibility later in this chapter.

What Do They Look Like?

What do diskettes **look** like? Well, *physically* they're square and as previously discussed, they come in two sizes, **5 1/4-inch** and **3 1/2-inch.** They also have three common features: *labels, read/write openings and write-protect notches.*

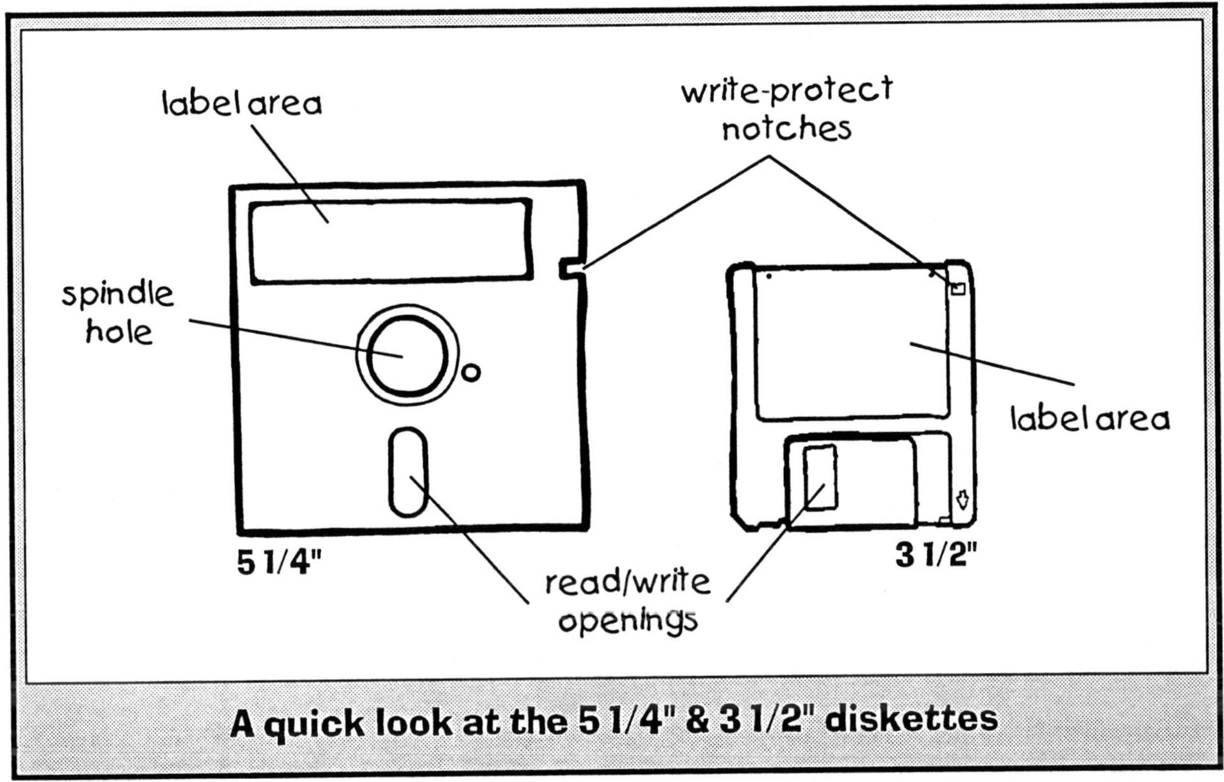

A quick look at the 5 1/4" & 3 1/2" diskettes

Labels

The labels *indicate the information/data* stored on the diskette. Software programs bought from stores have the labels *already printed* and put on the diskette. You'll make your own labels for the diskettes you use to store the information/data files you've created.

When you are making your labels, describe the disk's contents and put the date on the label, you know, *general information.* Always write on your disk labels *before* you attach the label to the disk. Writing on the label *after* it's on the disk can result in damage or loss of data due to the pressure your pen tip puts on the diskette.

Read/Write openings

This is the area where the *read/write heads* on the floppy disk drive can access the disk. As discussed previously, the floppy drive has a **read** (look at)/**write** (record) head similar to what a needle is to a record player. While the disk spins, the read/write head has access to the entire diskette through this opening.

Write-protect notch

This thing prevents you or anyone else from accidently or deliberately changing or erasing anything on the diskette. When your diskette is "*write-protected*" you **cannot** change, alter or delete anything on that diskette. You can't even accidentally reformat it. *You can* read and copy files from the diskette.

Write-protect your *original software program diskettes* and any diskettes that hold information that should not change. The write-protect notch is different on 5 1/4-inch and 3 1/2-inch diskettes. See **"Write-Protecting Diskettes"** in this section.

Diskette Storage Capacities

Each physical diskette size also has **varying storage capacities.** These various capacities are measured in terms of *kilobytes **(Kb)*** and *megabytes **(Mb)**,* (As explained earlier in Chapter 9). The following illustration gives you an idea of the different sizes and capacities of diskettes.

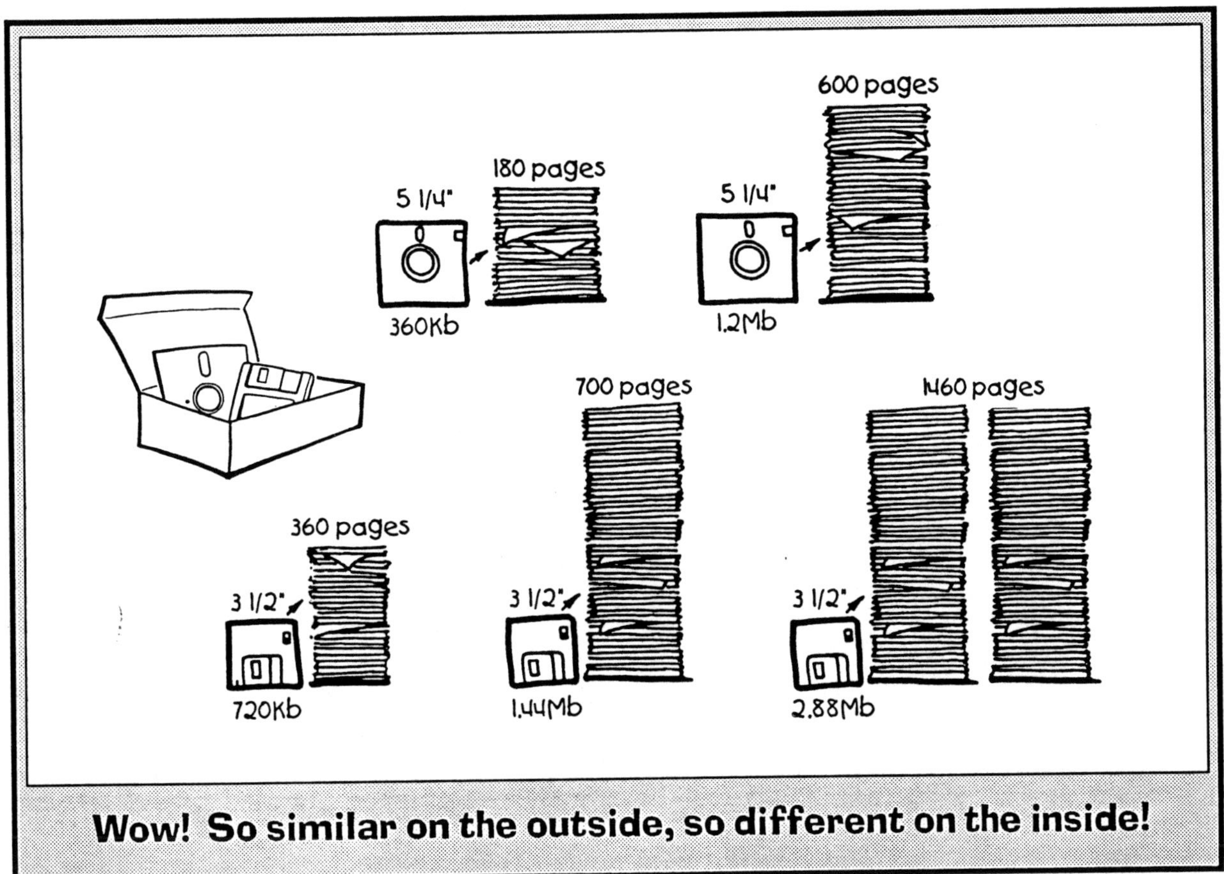

Wow! So similar on the outside, so different on the inside!

As you can see, there are **several types of diskettes** available for computers. When floppy diskettes were introduced back when IBM started making personal computers (1981) they were capable of storing only *160Kb* (That's about 80 pages of text.) of information. As technology increased disk storage capabilities, the amount of information a diskette could hold grew to what you see in the illustration.

Today, the most common floppy diskettes are the 1.2Mb, 5 1/4-inch diskette along with the 1.44Mb, 3 1/2-inch diskette, *but* there are also 360Kb, 5 1/4- inch diskettes along with 720Kb, 3 1/2-inch diskettes out there. **Why do you need this information?** Because... you have to have the right floppy diskette for your floppy disk drive type. **Huh?!**

Here's how it works (or doesn't work.) The **1.2Mb floppy disk drive** will read both *360Kb & 1.2Mb, 5 1/4-inch diskettes* but the **360Kb floppy disk drive** will only read the *360Kb diskettes*. If you put a 1.2Mb diskette into a 360Kb drive, IT WILL EXPLODE! Just kidding. It won't work. It'll give you some kind of error message like Track 1 is bad on the floppy.

Putting a 1.2Mb diskette into a 360Kb floppy disk drive is kind of like pouring a gallon of milk into a half-gallon container. There ain't enough room. Now... you can put a 360Kb diskette into a 1.2Mb drive. It'll work! That's like pouring a half-gallon of milk into a gallon container. There's plenty of room.

Check out the following illustration for a picture of *floppy disk drive* to *floppy diskette* capacity equivalents.

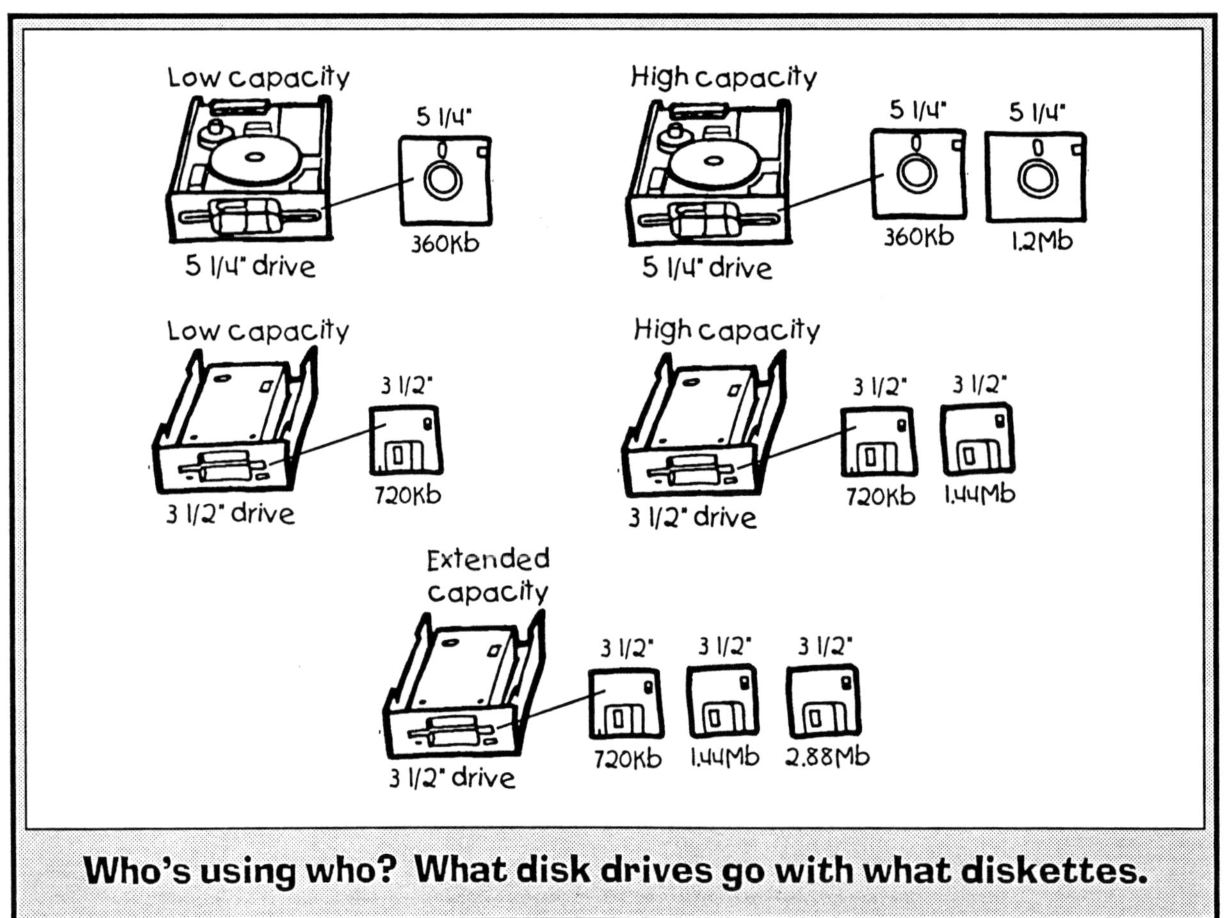

Who's using who? What disk drives go with what diskettes.

All computers have at least one floppy disk drive, with many systems incorporating the use of two floppy drives. Most of these systems using two floppy drives use both the 5 1/4-inch and 3 1/2-inch drives.

Here's A Tip!

If you are out shopping for an aftermarket floppy disk drive, be sure that you are getting the *high capacity* type. Even though most computers built in the last few years already incorporate these type of drives, you may encounter someone who got a *"good deal"* on low capacity drives and wants to pass that good deal on to you.

Remember! The high capacity drives can use the lower capacity floppy diskettes as well as the high capacity diskettes. Two for one!

Formatting (Preparing Storage Media)

Storage media disks must be **formatted** (prepared) before they can be used. This formatting process only needs to be performed on a disk once, although they can be reformatted. (Check your much loved DOS manual to reformat.)

In order to try to get you to understand what formatting is, we'd like you to picture the storage disk as a piece of *undeveloped land.* The operating software (DOS) is given the job of the land developer.

Before you can build on the land, you (DOS) gotta level the ground, move some trees, rocks and other debris. While leveling the the land you come across

some areas that you should not build on as well as some rocks and trees that cannot be removed. You (DOS) then mark those areas off as unbuildable.

Formatting a disk is similar. It prepares the surface of the disk to work with your operating system and makes the disk ready to accept data for storage. Using special operating software (DOS) instructions, the computer smoothes out a path on the disk and marks off bad areas so no data is stored there.

Avoid formatting any drives other than the "A" or "B" drives. Your hard drive, called the "C" drive (that makes it a drive *other than* "A" or "B",) will most likely be formatted when you receive your computer. If not, check with a qualified technical type of person or read your DOS manual **very carefully** before attempting to format your hard disk drive.

Formatting a disk erases all data previously stored on it. ***You have been warned!!!!!!!***

Formatting a Disk

The following is a *brief overview* of the **format** command, which is used to format disks. For more information on the format command ***refer*** to your DOS manual.

To format a diskette, use the **format** command followed by the drive letter of the drive (**"A"** or **"B"**) in which the diskette is inserted, followed by a colon (:). The command would look like this if you were working with a diskette in drive "A":

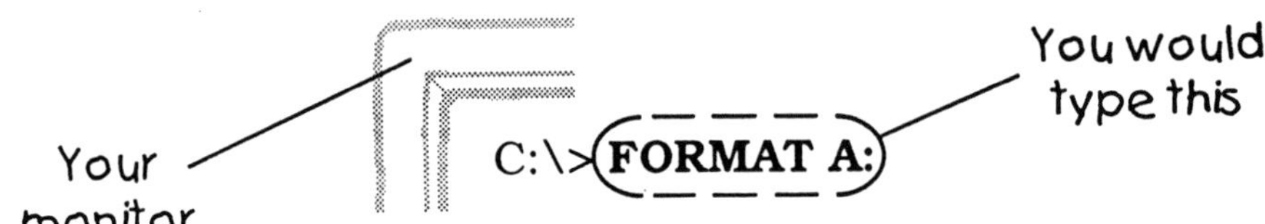

Now... press the key marked **Enter**. This instructs the computer to format the floppy diskette in drive "A." After pressing Enter, the computer will ask you to insert a disk into drive "A." You've already done that, so **press Enter again** and the disk begins formatting.

After the formatting is done, the computer will ask you if you want to enter a *"volume label"* for the disk. You can press ENTER to bypass this function (unless you want to electronically put a label on your diskette, *this is optional.*) It'll also ask you if you want to format another diskette. Press "Y" (yes) if you do, then remove the first diskette and put in another OR press "N" for no.

There are several other DOS commands for formatting high and low density diskettes in both 5 1/4 and 3 1/2 inch diskettes. See you DOS manual for these commands.

Write-Protecting Diskettes

Write-protecting your floppy disks **prevents** you, your computer, or anyone else from accidently or deliberately changing or erasing anything on the diskette. When your diskette is write-protected, you cannot change, alter or delete anything on that diskette. You can't even accidentally reformat it. *You can read and copy files from a write-protected diskette.*

Write-protect your original software program diskettes (if they are not already write-protected) and any diskettes that hold information that should not be changed.

The write-protect notch is different on 5 1/4 inch and 3 1/2 inch diskettes. Read the following write-protect rules.

Write-Protecting a 5 1/4-inch Diskette
To write-protect a 5 1/4 inch diskette, take one of those little sticky tabs that are on the same sheet that your diskette labels come on and cover

the *notch* on the disk. The notch is located on the *upper-right* side of the disk as you are holding the disk with the *label facing you* and the read/write opening kind of *pointing downward*. With that notch covered, the diskette is **write-protected**. You can't write to it but you can read from it. Look at the illustration below:

5 1/4" floppy: To write-protect or not to write-protect.

To **unwrite-protect** a 5 1/4-inch diskette, simply peel off the sticky tab you put on. Simple as that. Now you can write to that diskette as well as read and copy from it.

Write-Protecting a 3 1/2-inch Diskette

Don't look for a "notch" on the 3 1/2 inch diskette. *There ain't one.* To write-protect a 3 1/2 inch diskette, locate the square hole with the sliding tab on the *bottom-left* side of the disk with the *label facing you* and the read/write area *pointing upward*. **Move the tab**, so that a hole *shows through* the disk. You'll have to move the tab from the back side. If you can *see daylight* through the hole, your diskette is **write-protected**. You can't write to it but you can read from it. Check out the following illustration:

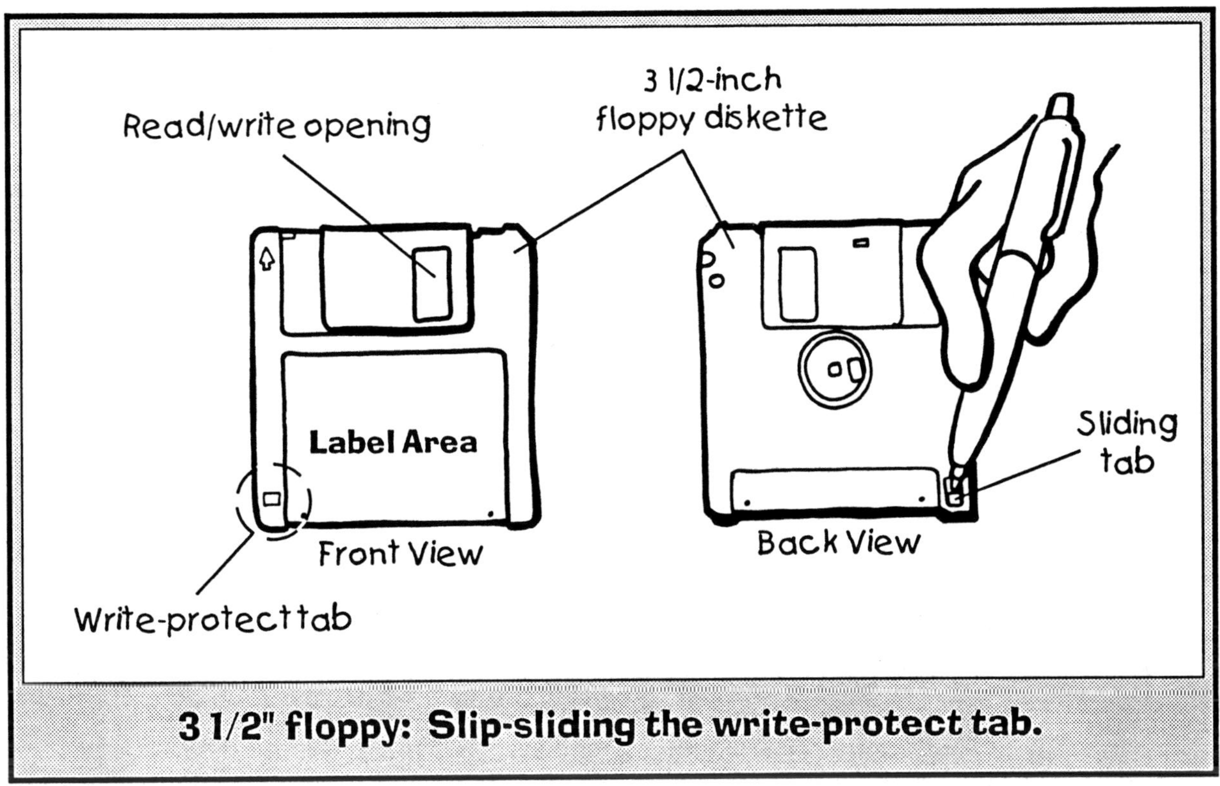

3 1/2" floppy: Slip-sliding the write-protect tab.

To **unwrite-protect** a 3 1/2-inch diskette, slide that tab to a position where the square hole is *no longer see through.* That's it. Now you can write to that diskette as well as read and copy from it.

Write-Protect Error Message

You *can't add information* to a diskette that is write-protected. If you try to do so, your diskette will melt inside the drive. Just kidding! You'll get an error message on your screen like "Write-protect error." This does not mean there is anything wrong with the disk. It just means it's not gonna let you copy anything to that disk. *It's protecting the disk.*

Along with the error message come the ever popular computer words, **Abort, Retry, Ignore?** At this point, if you *really* want to add to your protected diskette, you've got to take the disk out, *remove* or *slide* (whichever applies) the write-protect tab, put the disk back in the drive and press R (Retry) followed by the Enter key. Otherwise press A (Abort) then Enter.

How To Insert A Diskette

A diskette is not of much use to you unless it is ultimately inserted into the floppy disk drive. If the diskette is put in the wrong way, *it will not work.* The computer won't read it. You'll get a message that'll say that the disk is not ready for use. If this happens, take the disk out and put it back in the right way.

The right way? Yup! There is one right way and seven wrong ways to insert a floppy disk. Even experienced computer users sometimes insert diskettes incorrectly. Look at the illustrations and use the following guidelines to insure proper floppy disk insertion:

How to properly feed your 5 1/4" floppy drive.

Most diskettes have a *label*, or a place for a label, on the *top side*. With the
label side up, hold the edge closest to the label. Insert the opposite end into
the drive first. This edge has the read/write opening slot on the 5 1/4-inch
diskette and the sliding shutter door on the 3 1/2-inch diskette.

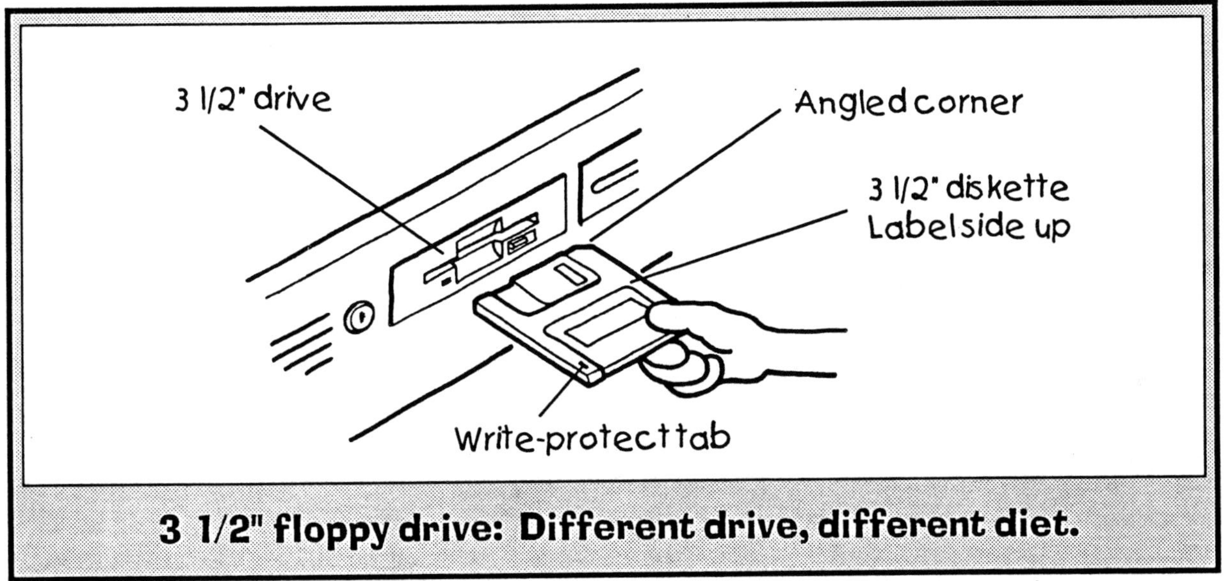

3 1/2" floppy drive: Different drive, different diet.

Once inside the drive, the diskette is in position for use when the *drive-door
latch* is closed. The drive-door latch applies only to the 5 1/4-inch diskette
drives. The 3 1/2-inch diskette pops in automatically. You'll know when it's
in. Trust me on this.

Remember diskettes come in two sizes: **5 1/4-inch**
and **3 1/2-inch**. Holes (slots) in the front
of the computer are made just for these
disks. You ain't gonna fit the 5 1/4-inch
disk into the 3 1/2-inch hole or vice-versa.
It's not gonna happen.

When you do find the right hole, put the *label side*
of your diskette facing up, the *write-protect notch/tab* will be
on the left and the *read/write opening* goes in the hole first.
(On the 5 1/4-inch drive, don't forget to close the door!)

Removing A Diskette

Removal of the diskettes from their drives is just the reverse motion of inserting the diskettes, *except...*

...the 5 1/4-inch diskette drive needs to have the drive-door latch opened before you can remove the diskette. The 3 1/2-inch diskette drive has a little "eject" button you need to push to pop the diskette out. That's it!

Take Care of Your Diskettes!
1) Do NOT touch disk surface.
2) Do NOT use alcohol cleaners to clean disk.
3) Do NOT use magnets around disks.
4) Do NOT bend disks.
5) Do NOT put heavy objects on disks.
6) Do NOT use rubber bands or paper clips.
7) Do NOT write on disks with pencil/ball point pen.
8) Do NOT use erasers on disks.
9) Do NOT use labels in layers.
10) Carefully insert disk in drive - do NOT force.
11) Keep disk in protective sleeve.
12) Store disks vertically (stand up) in their box.
13) Do NOT expose disk to excessive heat or sunlight.
14) Do NOT use diskettes for coasters. (See #5)

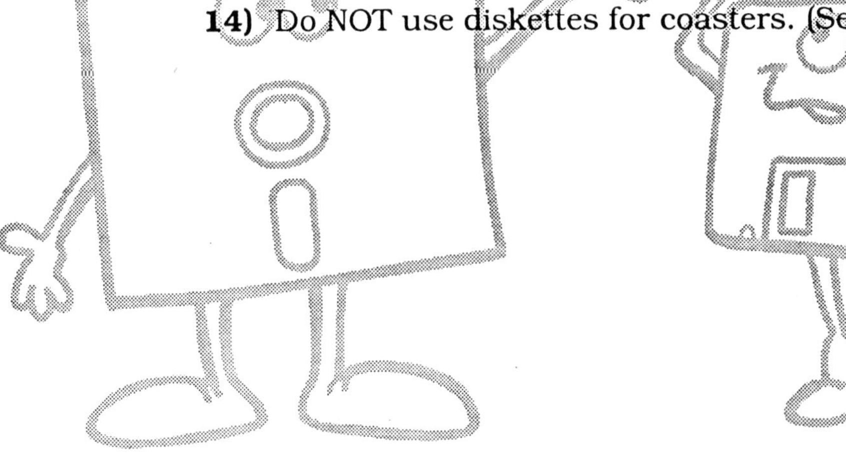

What Did You Learn?

Diskettes are **removable storage** media. They allow information to be *shared* with different computers. Floppy diskettes are convenient for sharing information and distributing software. Besides storing information, diskettes can *copy information* from the hard drive. They are availabe in **two sizes**: 5 1/2-inch and 3 1/2-inch with *varying storage capacity*. Through the read/write opening on the diskette, the floppy drive can **"read"** and **"write"** information on the diskette.

You also learned how to **protect** information on your diskette and how to **care** for your diskette.

Chapter 11

The Software

"Class, pay attention! There will be a test later."

So far we've told you about the "hardware" part of a computer. And all the hardware we've discussed that physically makes up the computer is *totally useless* on its own. To go from useless to *useful* a computer needs directions or instructions. **Something to tell it what to do.** That something is called **software**.

Software is to a computer what a teacher is to a student, what brains are to that teacher or student. One is useless without the other. Without being told what to do *(by the software)* the computer is nothing more than an expensive paper weight.

Software is not something you can touch and feel. Software comes on a diskette but the diskette itself is not the software. Software is the instructions that are magnetically encoded onto the diskette surface, kinda like how music is recorded on a tape cassette *or* how your personal banking information is put on that little brown magnetic strip on the back of your credit card. Same concept.

The are several different kinds of software, but as a user, you only need to know about the two major categories of software: *operating* (system) *software and applications* (program) *software.*

Operating (System) Software 

Probably the most important software on your computer is the *operating* (system) *software.* **Every** computer must use some type of operating software. Operating software *coordinates* the hardware and software interaction, letting you use your "application" software, along with devices such as your printer. In general, your operating system software has to be activated before you can use your applications software to make your computer do things like wordprocessing. Most computers are set up to do this automatically when you turn them on. *Activating the system software is called "booting up" the system.*

DOS: Your Translator

On most PC computers, the operating software is called DOS, *(rhymes with "boss")* or Disk Operating System. This is a computer program that was created by a company called Microsoft. Their name for this program is *Microsoft Disk Operating System* or, as the rest of the industry calls it, **MS-DOS.**

In 1981, when IBM released the first PC, IBM bought (licensed) DOS from Microsoft for use on the PC and called it **PC-DOS.** That's short for *Personal Computer Disk Operating System.* Nowadays, Microsoft sells (licenses)DOS to other IBM-PC compatible computer manufacturers and they label DOS using their own name, such as: Zeos DOS, Compaq DOS, Tandon DOS, etc. From the user's point of view, *they're pretty much the same,* providing the same commands and capabilities.

DOS helps to translate what you tell your computer into a language the computer can understand. DOS commands offer you a very powerful tool in the control of your computer. It offers commands that help to *organize* and *maintain* the information on your storage drives. With DOS, you can tell your computer to **print**, **copy** information from one area to another, **organize** and **sort** information, **erase** information, **start** your application software and much, much more.

Because they are so important, we will discuss some DOS commands in greater detail in Chapters 12 and 13. In this chapter we give you an *overview* of DOS and what it can do for your work on the computer.

What Does It Organize?

The information you work with is usually enclosed in **"files."** Some files contain letters and others might contain chapters from a book, like this one. Still other types of files contain pictures or even the software instructions that helped create a picture.

With the various types of files on a computer, organization is needed. So, *all files are organized* into groups called directories. You usually create a directory to group certain files that have something in common. It's similar to the way you might sort your laun-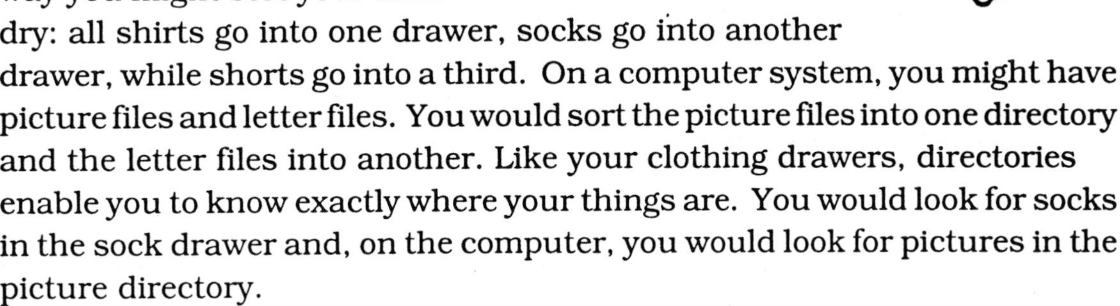
dry: all shirts go into one drawer, socks go into another drawer, while shorts go into a third. On a computer system, you might have picture files and letter files. You would sort the picture files into one directory and the letter files into another. Like your clothing drawers, directories enable you to know exactly where your things are. You would look for socks in the sock drawer and, on the computer, you would look for pictures in the picture directory.

The Prompt, What's in a Letter?

One letter of the alphabet that you are going to become **very familiar** with is the letter **"C."** "C" is the ID name for your main storage hard drive, where all of your software files are or will be stored. When you first turn on your computer, it will run through a few self checks and then end *(usually)* with the following "prompt."

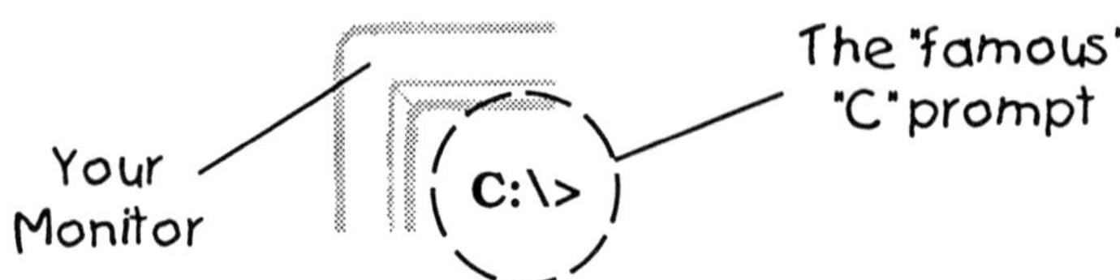

This prompt, fondly known as "the C prompt," is your operating system's (DOS's) way of saying "OK, here I am, tell me what to do." Whenever you see the C:\> prompt, you can issue one of the many DOS commands.

Take a note. (Or a letter.) The letters A, B, C, etc. in the prompt tells you which disk drive you're currently using.

The computer is now *ready* to accept your input. This means it's **time to type something** after the prompt. The text you type on the keyboard will appear on the screen right next to the prompt. At this point you should either be typing in DOS commands or names of programs. Sending the command to be processed is done by *pressing the Enter key.*

Error Messages at the Prompt

There are two error messages that commonly appear at the DOS prompt:

> **"File not found"** DOS will display this message when it successfully executes your command but cannot find the file name that you

specified in the command. ***Don't panic;*** you may have just typed the file name in incorrectly. *If this message appears,* make sure you are spelling the file name correctly. Also, check to see that you are in the right directory that contains that file.

"Bad command or file name" DOS will display this message when it can't find a command that matches the one you typed in at the prompt. Again, ***don't panic.*** If this happens, check your spelling to make sure you have spelled the command correctly. Also, check your current disk drive and directory.

For other error messages, refer to a DOS book or the DOS user's manual that came with your computer.

Looking at Your Files: TYPE Command

If you don't want to start up a program to view the contents of a file, the **TYPE** command can be helpful. You simply enter the TYPE command along with the name of the file you want to view. *For example,* to view the contents of a spreadsheet file called "INVOICE.123," you would type:

and press the Enter key. The contents of the file will then be displayed on the screen. If you want to print out the contents of the file you just viewed add the **PRN** (print) command.

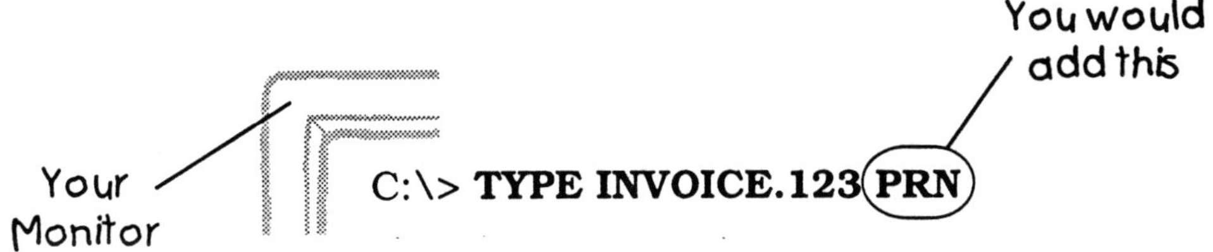

You may get some odd results when viewing some files. Program files usually contain different types of codes that may appear as gibberish when viewed with the TYPE command.

Viewing Your Directories: DIR Command

Probably the most commonly used DOS command is the one to look at the *directory* structure on your disk. *(A directory is like a folder in your computer where you store files that are like or related to one another when you save them.)* This DOS command, called **DIR** (that's short for DIRectory), lists all the files in a directory and all of the subdirectories within that directory.

Let's say you are in a directory called *Accounts* and you wanted to know which accounts files are included in the directory. To get a directory list you would type:

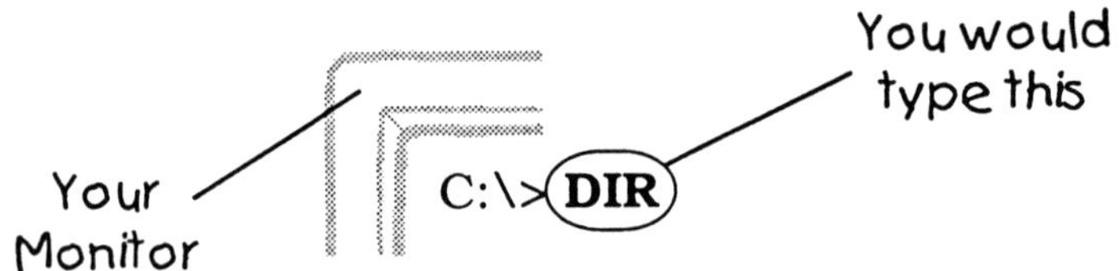

and the computer would give you a list of files included it that directory. In the nex chapter, we talk a little more about listing directories.

Keeping Track of Time: DATE and TIME

All computers have a **clock** that is powered by a battery inside the computer. This small battery will keep the current **date** and **time** *even if the computer is turned off.* The computer uses the date and time feature to keep track of the date and time when each information file was last updated. This

feature becomes important for tracking and security purposes. For example, you can tell if anyone has changed a file while you were gone by looking at the file's date and time stamp.

DATE and **TIME** are DOS commands that can be used to either set or check the date and time that the computer has registered. To set a new time or date, you just type "DATE" or "TIME" at the prompt, press the ENTER key, then type in the new information.

For example, to set a new date, you would first type the word **DATE** at the "C" prompt:

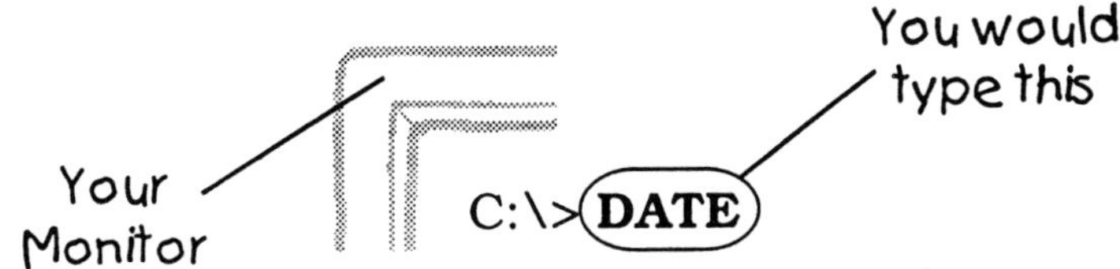

and the computer will display its current setting, like so;

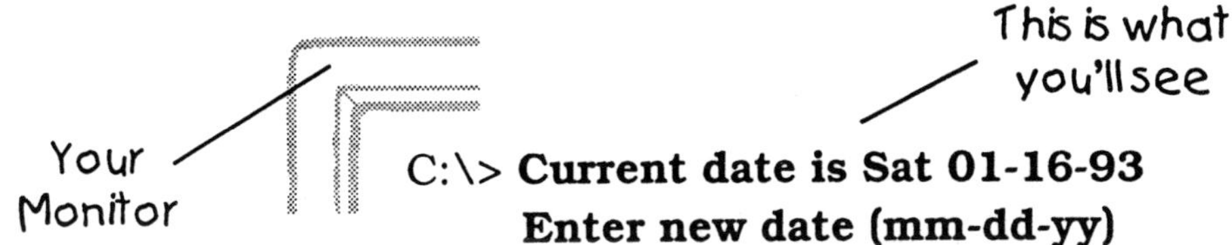

(Of course, it may not be that exact date, that just happens to be my daughter's birthday.) At this point, *you could* enter a new date or simply press Enter if the computer has the right date. If you do enter a new date, you must first type two digits for the month, then the day, then the year. In that order. *Remember* the dashes between each set of numbers.

The **TIME** command works very similar to the DATE command. To set a new time, you would type the word TIME at the "C" prompt and the computer would display something similar to what you saw for the date.

At that point, *you could* enter a new time or simply press Enter if the computer had the right time. If you do enter a new time, you must first type the *hour*, then the *minute*, then the *second*, and then (if you're really exact) the hundredths of a second. *Remember* to put colons (:) between each number in the time. Most people do not bother with typing in seconds or hundredths and that's alright with DOS.

Depending on the version of DOS you are using, time may be kept in **military** or **am/pm** time. For DOS 4.0 and later, you can type an "a" for *am* or "p" for *pm* after your time to indicate whether it is morning or evening time. For versions of DOS **before** 4.0, time is kept in military time. So if it's 1:00 p.m., earlier versions of DOS will tell you it's 13:00:00:00.

What Version?

DOS has *version numbers.* The version of DOS on your computer determines what kind of commands are included. Each new version of DOS includes *more features* than the last. To date, there have been five major versions of DOS released, numbered 1 through 5. Each of these major releases have also had their own little minor releases (versions *within* versions), like DOS 1.0, 1.1, 2.0, 2.1, etc. (The major release being separated from the minor release by a period.)

To find out which version of DOS you system is using, type **VER** at the "C" prompt:

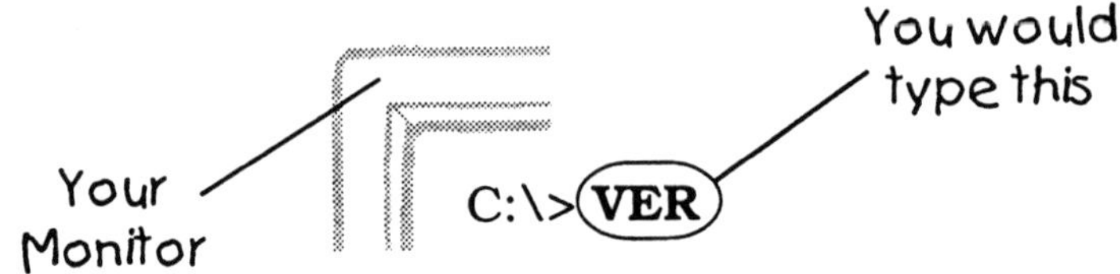

then press Enter. DOS then displays its name and version number.

Installing the Operating System

The operating system is *software.* Just like all other software, the operating system must be installed before your computer can run it. These days, when you buy your computer, the operating system is usually already installed. *If you've got to install the operating system yourself,* follow the installation instructions referred to in the DOS manual or check your system documentation.

Software That Makes It Easier

Many software developers have spent time creating programs that are easier to use. Like DOS, many software programs have required you to enter information through prompts and commands. Newer programs are more **graphical** and use symbols, such as **icons** and **windows**, to display files and directories.

Remember the commands you type at the DOS "C" prompt? Well, *in a graphical system* you don't type commands. You **"select"** them from the **"menus"** that pull down from the top of the screen. And instead of looking at a directory list of files, you will see a window full of little icons. These new programs use a *Graphical User Interface* (or GUI). GUI's have pull-down menus, display windows, icons, and dialogue boxes. You can interact with any of these elements by using a mouse to point and select options.

As we mentioned in an earlier chapter, one very popular graphical program is called **Windows**. Windows, developed by the Microsoft Corporation, is really not *just* another software program. The introduction of Microsoft Windows 3.1 has a started a new trend towards creating more graphical programs that easier to use than older programs. Since you are bound to hear about Windows in your work with computers, we cover a few things about it in this section. Read on.

Windows... "What's That?"

Microsoft Windows is a **graphical user interface** or a GUI (pronounced "gooey") that changes the way you interface or "talk" to your computer. *Instead* of using **typed** DOS commands, Windows uses pictures and symbols, called **icons**, to make it easier for you to use your computer.

These icons represent programs. This visual approach enables you to *point* to an *icon* with your mouse, then *click* (push the button on the mouse), which then starts the program. For example, pointing and clicking on the calendar picture in your windows program will bring a calendar to your screen. <u>That simple</u>.

Windows lets you run *more than one program at once,* each in its own window, as long as your system has enough memory. Switching between programs is as simple as pointing and clicking the mouse. With Windows, you can instantly transfer data from one program to another, as in putting text that you might have typed in a word processing program into a desktop publishing program. (We did that with this book!)

Windows works best when it's running Windows-specific programs, such as *WordPerfect for Windows, Word for Windows, MS-Works for Windows, Quicken for Windows,* and so on. **It can run other DOS programs** as well, but you won't get all the fancy Window screens. Those programs will just appear in full-screen size. No graphical interface. Like you never ran it through the Windows program.

To add a little more, the Windows package comes with several accessories. These include a *clock, appointment calendar, note pad, calculator, card file,* and a couple of *games.* Once it's set up, Windows becomes simply automatic, easy to use (easier than DOS, but what wouldn't be?), and kinda fun.

Summing Up Windows

You should really talk with your reseller about the benefits that Windows can offer. It is a **powerful** and **useful** software program. More and more software programs are becoming available to be used with Windows. You need to understand Windows to make sure it's worth the investment. **DOS is required for use with Windows.** So, you *don't* need to give up the standard command style interface to use Windows.

Application (Program) Software 

Software that lets you perform useful tasks, such as creating a letter (**wordprocessing** software,) making a mailing list (**database** software,) create a newsletter (**desktop publishing** software,) is application software.

Choosing the right application software is very important. To choose the correct software, you should analyze your computing needs. Will you use the computer for *home* or *business.* Games? Maybe a combination of these. Ask yourself *"What do I want my computer to do?"* Do you want to use it as a typewriter, a general ledger, or maybe a typesetting machine? Choose the application that will accomplish your goals. Ask your friends how they met their application software needs. What do they use?

In this chapter we describe some of the most popular types of application software and how they can be of use to you.

Word Processing (writing stuff) Software

The *most commonly used* application software is word processing software. And when you mix word processing application software with a computer 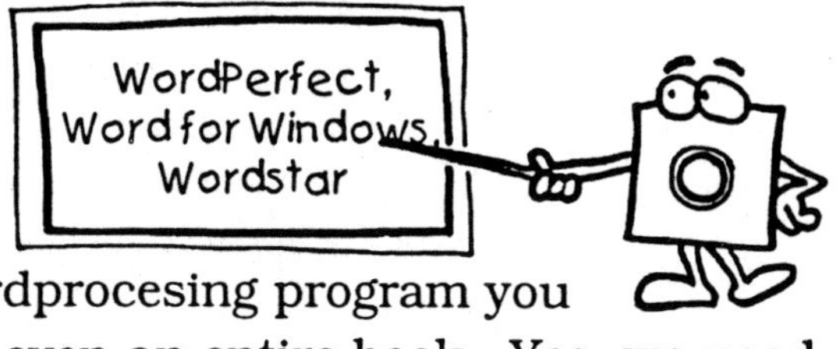

you get **super typewriter!** With a wordprocesing program you can create *letters, resumes, memos,* or even an entire book. Yes, we used word processing software to write this book.

With a word processor you compose text on you computer keyboard just like you would on a typewriter keyboard. The difference is, with a word processor, things like correcting mistakes and making changes are made electronically on the screen before you print the document. With a type writer you make these changes with a bottle of white out (correction fluid) after you print it out. *Which would you rather do?*

Some consider word processing software to be merely a replacement for the typewriter. Hah! That's like comparing a typewriter to pencil and eraser. Word processing has many advantages over the typewriter. First, it can *make changes to text* easily and quickly. It can also **move, add, copy,** or **erase** information in just a few steps. Word processors also let you *format* your document, allowing you to use different *fonts* and character *sizes.* Word processing programs provide many tools for "editing" your writing.

Most word processing programs also have *spell checkers.* The spell checker reviews your document and stops on any misspelled words. You then have the option to correct the spelling yourself or choose from a list of similarly spelled words that the software shows you.

There are lots of different word processor programs available today. Their costs and capabilities do differ. The following is a small sampling of what's available these days:

<u>Software Name</u>	<u>Company</u>
WordPerfect	WordPerfect Corp.
Word	Microsoft Corp.
Word for Windows	Microsoft Corp.
Wordstar	Micropro Corp.
Professional Write	Software Publishing Corp.
Multimate	Ashton-Tate

Spreadsheet (calculating stuff) Software

Spreadsheet software was designed to help you **organize numbers** and complete **mathematical calculations.** On your screen you'll see an electronic version of an accountant's (spreadsheet) worksheet. Using

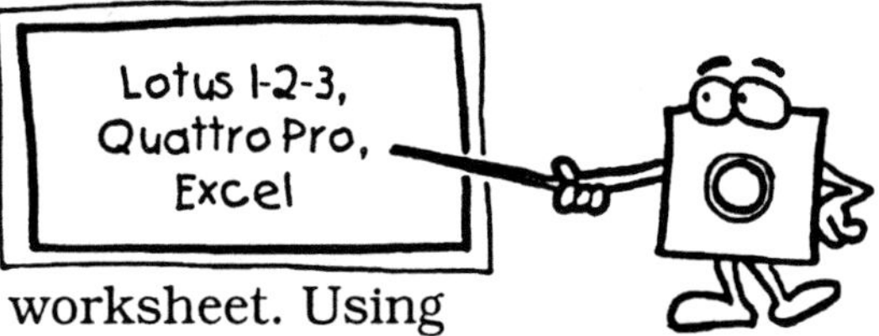

a spreadsheet, you can just about toss out your calculator or adding machine. *Addition, subtraction, multiplication, division, percentages,* and other mathematical operations are all specialties of a spreadsheet software program.

A spreadsheet program shows *columns* and *rows,* much like the typical accountant's ledger sheet. Unlike the accountant's paper worksheet whose actual paper size is fixed, the electronic spreadsheets "working area" is almost endless, letting you work with over a million values. *Wow!*

Spreadsheets are used quite a bit to perform *"what if"* analysis. Because these spreadsheet programs can really zip through complex number calculations that use thousands of values, you can determine "what" the result would be, "if" you changed one or more values. And it does it pretty darn quick, too!

Also, in addition to giving you these values in numbers form, many of these spreadsheet programs display your data on charts and graphs, giving you an easy look at what's happening.

Just as the case is with other software programs, spreadsheet software is available from several different companies. Again, their costs and capabilities can and do differ. Here's a sample of what is available:

<u>Software Name</u>	<u>Company</u>
Lotus 1-2-3	Lotus Corp.
Excel	Microsoft Corp.
Quattro Pro	Borland International

Database Management (Information Organizer) Software

Everybody keeps **lists** of one sort or another, right? Maybe you have a list of family birthdays. A list of customers. How about a list of people you don't like? What's the name of *that* list???

In simple terms a database ain't nothing more than an **organized collection** of those lists you have. A phone book, your recipe box, an address book *(little black book?)*, consider these a type of database.

A database software program helps you *create, organize, store,* and later *retrieve* lists of information. Using a database program, you can sort your information by **specific field,** such as name, or city, or maybe by phone number. The information is immediately accessible to be updated, printed, or included in reports.

The following is a sample list of popular database programs, and as is standard with software these days, costs and capabilities will differ.

<u>Software Name</u>	<u>Company</u>
DBase	Ashton-Tate (Borland)
RBase	MicroRim
Paradox	Borland International
FoxBase	Fox Software

Accounting (Checking & Bookkeeping) Software

Accounting software packages for personal and small business use are fairly inexpensive (under $100 bucks), very useful, and are relatively easy to use. Typically, they **imitate your checkbook** with additional

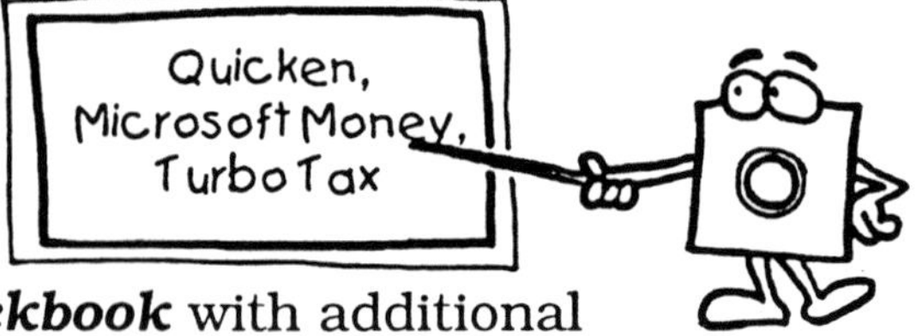

features such as tracking several bank accounts (checking & savings), cash, credit cards, assets & liabilities.

These programs can also generate cash flow reports, monthly budget reports, and other types of reports. Things like payroll, profit and loss statements, payable and receivables, can also be generated through these type of programs. Some programs listed under accounting software do your **taxes** for you, too.

There are several accounting software packages available today that are very useful for home or office. Here is a list of some popular packages:

<u>Software Name</u>	<u>Company</u>
Quicken	Intuit
Peachtree	Peachtree Software
Managing Your Money	MECA
DacEasy Accounting	DacEasy
TurboTax	ChipSoft

Desktop Publishing (Making it "Look good") Software

Desktop publishing (DTP) is a combination of **word processing** and **graphics** software. It is therefor used to create documents to be printed,

such as *this book*, magazines, newsletters, catalogs, advertisements, annual reports, brochures and the list goes on.

It allows you to take text created in a word processor and mix it up with graphics created in a graphics program and move it around any way you please. You can change type styles and sizes along with the spacing between characters (kerning) and the spacing between lines (leading) at will. There are lots of things you can do with this very powerful software. Maybe that's why it is *so expensive.* ($300. - $700.)

This book is an example of a product created using desktop publishing software. The actual writing (typing) of this book was done using a word processor *(WordPerfect 5.1)* and then those text files were "imported" (electronically pulled into) the desktop publishing software *(Pagemaker 4.0)*.

Once inside the Pagemaker software, we created the *look* of the book. How *wide* should the columns of text be? Should the right margins be straight or ragged? What type style and type size should the chapter titles be? What should page numbers look like? What about white space? Use to be, this type of work was sent out to be done by graphic artists and typesetters. An *expensive* and *time consuming* process.

Desktop publishing software gives the user the ability to create *professional* looking documents right on their own computers. You get to see what the document will look like right on the screen. This is called **WYSIWYG** (pronounced wizzy-wig) an acronym for *what-you-see-is-what-you-get*. What you see on the screen is close to what you get when it's printed.

As mentioned before, desktop publishing software is not cheap. Plan on spending several hundred dollars to get a good program. Here are some names of popular DTP (Desktop Publishing) software:

<u>Software Name</u>	<u>Company</u>
PageMaker	Aldus
Ventura Publisher	Xerox
PFS:First Publisher	Software Publishing

Graphics (drawing pictures) Software

A picture is worth 6,000 bytes (a thou sand words). This old saying works with desktop publishing. Add some pictures to your newsletter, annual report, brochure. Bring it to life. This is what graphics software

lets you do. Graphics software is an extension of desktop publishing software.

Create your own graphics or use the electronic *clip art* (predrawn ready-made drawings on disks) provided by some software packages. Software companies sell disks containing clip art for just about every profession.

Along with the available clip art, graphic software provides you with a number of *tools* to be endlessly creative. These tools allow you to draw *lines, curves, rectangles, circles, add text, re-shape text, outline text, duplicate, reposition* or *reverse images*. The list goes on.

There are many graphic software packages available. The *price range* will definitely vary in this category, depending on the capabilities of the software. Here's a list of a few:

<u>Software Name</u>	<u>Company</u>
CorelDRAW!	Corel Systems
Harvard Graphics	Software Publishing
Micrografx Designer	Micrografx
Arts & Letters	Computer Support
Powerpoint	Microsoft

CAD (Computer-Aided Design) Software

T-square, triangle, compass, template and mechanical pencils. Tools of the trade for **architects, engineers, draftsmen, technical illustrators** and **product designers.** Used to be, *not anymore.*

Computer-aided design software has put all the *tools of the trade* on your computer. The computer screen and mouse become the drawing board and pencil, respectively. Instead of drawing something by hand, and then later redrawing it, by hand, the user draws the object on the computer screen using the mouse. Once the object is drawn, the CAD software lets you *change* the object's size, *merge* the object with other objects, or even *rotate* the object for viewing from a different perspective.

Most CAD software programs, ***intended for use by professionals***, are very sophisticated. And some are **very** expensive, although relatively inexpensive CAD software packages are available.
Here's the names of a few:

<u>**Software Name**</u>	<u>**Company**</u>
Autocad	Autodesk
Autosketch	Autodesk
Generic CADD	Generic Software
DesignCAD	American Small Business Co.

Communications (Computer Phone Talk) Software

Computers talking with computers.
By phone? ***How?*** *Communications software* (and a modem.)

Communications software allows you to use your computer to communicate with other computers *over telephone lines.* By using the telephone lines to communicate, you can use your computer to do stuff like shop, make airline reservations, do your banking, or a whole bunch of other fun things. *(Some not so fun like, pay bills.)* Send and receive text (i.e., love/hate letters) to and from another computer down the hall *or* around the world.

Some names of popular communications software:

<u>**Software Name**</u>	<u>**Company**</u>
Carbon Copy Plus	Microcom
PROCOMM Plus	Datastorm Technologies
Prodigy	Prodigy Services Company

Educational (Get Smart) Software

Learn education's three basic skills...
Reading, writing and arithmetic.

Watch out! Computer literacy is fast becoming the *fourth.* Computers have *tremendously* enhanced instruction in all of these critically important learning skills.

The number of educational software programs available for computers these days is endless. *Reading, spelling, writing, grammar, elementary math, advanced math, history, geography, chemistry, earth science, foreign language,* the list goes on.

Whatever you're interested in learning, you can probably find software to help you along. Check with your local software dealer for a list of available educational software. In the meantime here's a few:

<u>**Software Name**</u>	<u>**Company**</u>
Reader Rabbit	The Learning Co.
Kids Math	Great Wave Software
Reading Tutor	Optimum Resource, Inc.

Entertainment (Let's Play Games!) Software

If you think computer's are all work and no play, *think again.* Computers can be **FUN!** There are literally hundreds of software programs available to entertain you. Sports games, war games, board games, or fantasy games - entertainment software can provide you with *hours of fun* and adventure. Here's *just three* of literally hundreds of games:

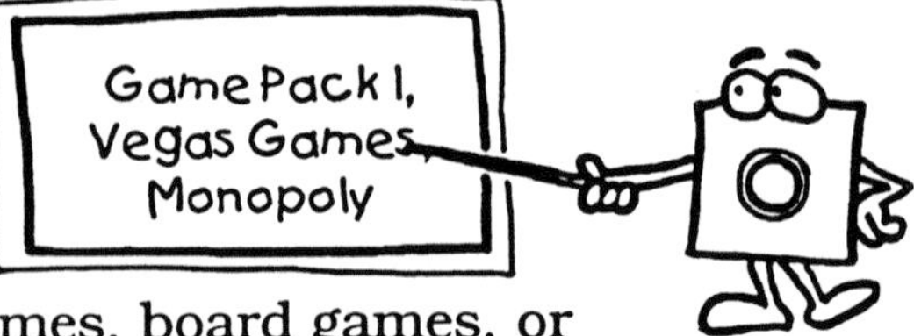

<u>Software Name</u>	<u>Company</u>
Game Pack 1	The Software Toolworks
Vegas Games	New World Computing
Monopoly Deluxe	Virgin Games, Inc.

Watch Out! Some of these games can be habit forming. We suggest that you do not use game software on the office computer *unless* you're the boss **or** your game program has a "boss" button. The boss button is a key you hit when the boss walks in. The monitor flashes a phony work screen that gives the impression your working. .

What Did You Learn?

We provided you with an overview of the most important software on your computer system - **the operating system**. On most PC computers, this operating system is called "DOS," for *disk operating system.*

DOS allows you to view the contents of your hard drive and provides a variety of *maintenance* tasks. Most of your work with DOS takes place through the system, or **C:\> prompt**. New software programs are beginning to move away from the tradi tional command prompt style.

Microsoft Windows uses a *graphical, visual* interface to perform many of the same functions as DOS. The visual elements of Windows, which include *menus, icons* and *window display* screens, provide an easier way to interact with your computer.

Take time to investigate what you want to do with your computer. When you understand your computer needs you can decide what kind of application software is best for you. Application software allows you to be productive on the com puter in many different ways. With software, you can *write, publish,* develop a balanced *budget, communicate* with comput-ers over phone lines, *get educated,* and even play *games.*

There are many software developers competing for your business in all areas of application software. Ask around to find out who is using what and why. Usually the most popular software is popular for a good reason. It works well for the majority of the people.

Chapter 12

Working With Directories

A hard disk drive provides the ability to *store large amounts of information* that your computer can access quickly and easily. This large storage area gives you the capability to store your **software** and your **information files** in one place rather than on several diskettes. One location holding thousands of pages of information needs organization. In this chapter we tell you about the disk operating system (DOS) commands that help you organize the information on your hard drive.

Hard disk drive; Organizing that thing.

Directories

DOS solves the organization problem by providing you with a way to categorize information on your hard disk. You create **directories** that contain *similar types of information.* For example, you can create a directory that contains *writing files* and another directory that contains *accounting files.* You will know to look in the writing directory for word processing files and in the accounting directory for banking information. Files can be found more quickly when grouped into directories.

Like Sorting Your Laundry

This method of organizing is used in many situations. *In fact*, you probably use it each week when you do laundry. We all use some kind of method to sort clothes when we do laundry. You may put all of your shorts in one pile, your shirts in another, and your socks in still another pile. **What are you doing?** You're *categorizing* your wardrobe so that each piece of clothing is in a pile with other common types of clothing.

Organizing your "stuff" so you know where to find it later.

The idea behind sorting **laundry** is convenience. The idea behind organizing your **hard drive** is also conveinience.

When you wake up in the morning you don't want to sort through a mixture of shorts, shirts, and socks *(although some of us do)*. You want to go to the shorts drawer to find a pair of shorts, then to the shirt drawer to find shirts, and so on. Sorting your clothing makes life a little easier.

Now that you're so organized, you can play computer games!

How Directories are Organized

Although you can create and organize the files and directories the way you want, there is always a *main directory* called the **root directory**. Every directory under the root is considered a **subdirectory**. On the next page we show you an example of how a law office might organize its hard drive.

Your *starting point* is the root directory, *your original pile of laundry.* This is where all the subdirectories branch from. The next level in the directory tree example separates into different software programs. You create a **DOS** subdirectory for DOS software files, **WORD** for word processing software files, and **123** for spreadsheet software files.

In looking at the WORD (word processing) subdirectory, you realize that your business creates a lot of contracts for different clients. You want to be able to group all your contracts in one subdirectory, called **CONTRACT**.

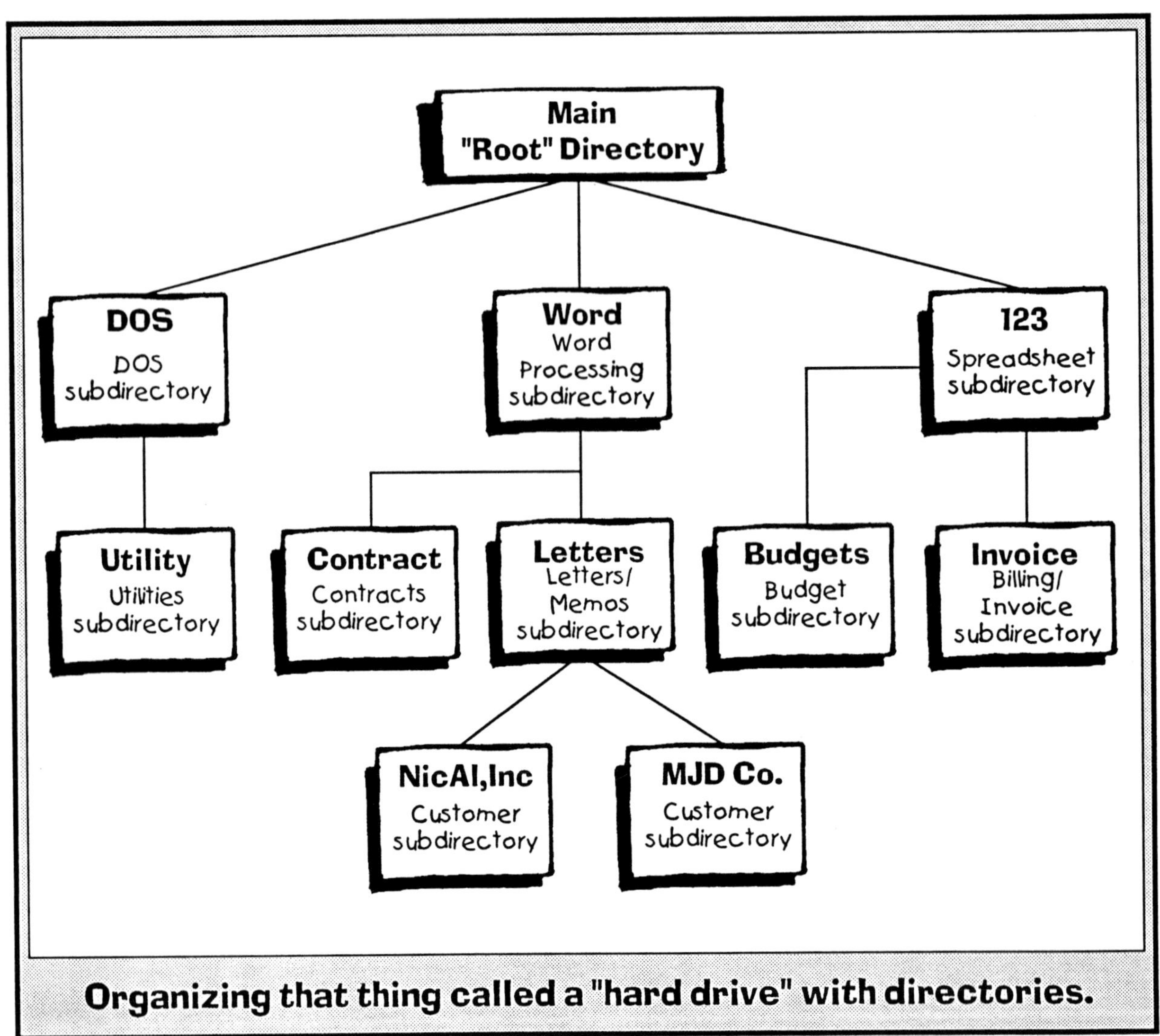

Organizing that thing called a "hard drive" with directories.

Most businesses also type many *letters* and *memos* using word processing software. To make sure letters and memos are separated from the contracts, you also create the **LETTERS** subdirectory to store all of the miscellaneous letters and memos.

Finally, your two top customers, **NicAl, Inc.** and **MJD Company**, have asked you to keep a copy of all written communication. In order to easily find this information, you create a subdirectory for each customer called Nical, Inc. and MJD Co.

There is **no limit** to the number of directories you can have, except a logical one. In other words you want to make sure that you categorize information into directories that *make sense.*

When naming a directory you must follow a few simple rules. The primary rule is that the name consists of a maximum of *eight* (8) *characters.* We advise that you use a directory name that indicates the *type of files* it contains. For example, we named the word processing subdirectory "WORD." We will show you how to create subdirectories later in this chapter.

Going Down the Path

You can organize information into directories. You saw a typical model for a law office directory tree in the last section. But how do you *access* information in each directory? Is there a way to move among directories to **find your way** to the information you are looking for?

To answer these questions, you need to understand the idea of **pathnames**. Every directory has a pathname. A pathname indicates all of the preceding directories that you must travel through to reach a specific directory or file. In other words, *a pathname is a* **road map** *or set of directions to a specific directory.* Here's a pathname example:

    C:\> WORD\LETTERS

This is how it breaks down:

C:	The drive letter
C:\>	The root directory on drive C
C:\> WORD	The WORD subdirectory on drive C
C:\> WORD\LETTERS	The LETTERS subdirectory under the WORD subdirectory

As you will note, the **backslash** (\) symbol in each pathname indicates the *separation* of different directory names. It is *also* the symbol for the *root directory*. In later sections of this chapter, we show you how to navigate your directory structure using pathnames.

What's In a (file)Name?

Directories serve one main purpose: *to group common files.* Files are the lifeblood of your work on the computer. Everything you write, draw, or create on the computer is eventually stored in a file that has a unique name. We will discuss files in more detail in the next chapter. For now, we will discuss how file names help further organize your directory structures.

The entire file name consists of two parts. The actual **name** consists of a maximum of *eight* (8) *characters* and a *three-letter* **extension**. The extension name is not mandatory when naming a file. In fact, you may find many files without them.

As a rule, you should give a file a *logical name* based on its contents. Giving a name of **INVOICE.MJD** to a file that contains *invoice* information for MJD Co. makes its contents clear. This will enable you to find the file even if you forget the name. This does happen, believe it.

The Current Directory

DOS commands take effect within what is called the **current directory.** This directory is the last directory named in the pathname of the prompt. If you are not in the directory where you want to perform a particular DOS command, then you will have to use a pathname in the DOS command. This pathname points to the correct directory. The following section *will help to clarify* directories and pathnames even more.

Moving Between Directories (CD Command)

This section describes the **CD** (Change **D**irectory) command. Remember, each directory has a *specific path* that must be followed in order to be accessed. We're gonna show you how to move through these paths

What It Looks Like

In order to change directories, you specify the CD command at the C:\> prompt by typing "**CD**" and then the pathname of the directory you want to change to. For example, the following command changes the drive access to the WORD directory.

> C:\> **CD WORD**

__Example.__ Using the directory tree shown at the beginning of this chapter, let's say you wanted to get to the **NicAl** subdirectory. Starting from the root directory, you would use the **CD** command until you reached the NicAl subdirectory. You follow these steps, *pressing* the Enter key after each one. Note that the ***prompt will change*** as you issue more CD commands.

<u>**You type**</u>	<u>**What happens?**</u>
C:\> **CD WORD**	Moves you to **WORD** subdirectory
C:\WORD> **CD LETTERS**	Moves you to **LETTERS** subdirectory
C:\WORD\LETTERS> **CD NICAL**	Moves you to **NICAL** subdirectory

After all of these steps, the following prompt appears, showing that you are in the NicAl subdirectory. The directory path that you took to get there is also shown.

> C:\WORD\LETTERS\NICAL>

Moving Directly To A Directory: A Short Cut

You do not have to use three CD commands to get to the NICAL subdirectory. *There is a faster way.* Using a pathname, you could combine all of the above steps into one command that looks like the following:

> **C:\> CD WORD\LETTERS\NICAL**

This command moves you clear from the root directory to the NICAL subdirectory. You can see that you can use the **CD** command to move to directories either one directory at a time or by specifying a pathname to move in one step. This option is true with *most* directory management commands in DOS.

A Couple of Other CD Commands

The CD command with **a slash**

> **C:\> CD**

takes you **back** to the root directory from any subdirectory.

The CD command with **two periods** (..) after it

> **C:\> CD..**

takes you back one directory in the structure. For example, if you were in the NICAL directory, it would take you back to LETTERS.

HEY! **WAKE UP!**

I know *firsthand* that this stuff is **very boring**...
...but you're probably gonna need it, so pay attention!

Making A Directory (MD Command)

Every directory on your hard drive has to be created using the **MD** (**M**ake **D**irectory) command. When you make a directory you need to use a name that gives you an idea of the type of files it contains.

What it Looks Like

The MD command is simple to use. First you type **MD** and then the pathname of the directory you want to create. The following MD command would create a WORD directory as a *subdirectory* of the root directory:

```
C:\> MD WORD
```

You need to *make sure you know* where you are in the directory structure when using MD. The directory you make automatically becomes a *subdirectory* of your current directory.

> ***Example.*** We'll use the directory structure of the law office to explain how the first few directories were created. In this example we start from the root directory. *Remember* to press the Enter key after each step. Note, that the prompt changes as you submit more commands.

You type	What happens?
C:\> **MD WORD**	Creates **WORD** subdirectory
C:\> **CD WORD**	*Changes* to **WORD** subdirectory
C:\WORD> **MD LETTERS**	Creates **LETTER** subdirectory
C:\>WORD\LETTERS> **MD NICAL**	Creates **NICAL** subdirectory

Removing A Directory (RD Command)

A time will come when you want to remove a directory using the (RD) **R**emove **D**irectory command. For example, if NicAl Inc. is no longer a customer, you will probably want to make a copy of all the information files in that directory, put it on diskette, and store it in a safe place for historical purposes. Then you can *remove* that directory so it doesn't clutter up your hard drive.

RD only works if there are no files or subdirectories within the directory you want to remove. This feature of RD helps prevent accidental removal of directories and files contained in the directory.

What It Looks Like

To use the RD command type **RD** at the C:\> prompt, then the pathname of the directory you want to remove. The following command would remove the WORD directory:

C:\> **RD WORD**

Before you use RD, you must position yourself in the directory just above the directory you want to remove. Also, the directory you want to remove must *not* have any files on it. We will explain how to delete files in the next chapter.

Listing Directories (DIR Command)

It is *very important* in computing to know what files are stored in on your hard drive. To obtain a list of files in a specific directory, you use the **DIR** (DIRectory) command. As with other directory management commands, DIR works in either the current directory *or* through the use of pathnames.

The DIR command **shows the following** information:

1) *Pathname* of the directory for which you are getting a listing
2) *Names of files* in the directory
3) *Names of subdirectories* branching from the directory. Noted by **<DIR>**
4) *Size* of each file in kilobytes
5) *Date* and *time* that each file was last updated

146

What It Looks Like?

The DIR command can be used by itself or with a pathname. Typing DIR by itself gives you a listing of the files in the current directory. Using a pathname will list files for the directory specified in the pathname. For example, the following command would list files in the WORD directory on drive C:

> C:\> **DIR C:\WORD**

**Example.** The following are a few more examples of how the DIR command is used.

You type   **What happens?**

C:\> **DIR**	Root directory
C:\> **DIR C:\WORD\LETTERS**	LETTERS subdirectory
C:\WORD> **DIR**	WORD subdirectory
C:\> **DIR A:**	Root directory on drive A:

Options Used With DIR

The DIR command has _several options_ that allow you to alter the appearance of the directory listing. We list the command and then explain what it does. Note that these options contain a **forward slash (/)** on the same key that has the question mark, unlike the previous commands that contained a backslash.

DIR/P

The **/P** stands for pause. In this command you request that the listing be shown only one screenful (or page) at a time. Such a listing is helpful when the list _(directory)_ is too long.

DIR/W

The **/W** stands for wide. When this directory screen comes up, it gives you a list of filenames only in five columns across the screen.

DIR/O

Putting the **/O** after the DIR command will give you the directory listing in alphabetical order. I guess "O" stands for order.

DIR A: (or B:)

DIR followed by the letter of a floppy drive, **"A"** or **"B"**, along with the colon (:)gives you a list of the files in that floppy drive. Be sure to have the disk in the floppy drive *before* you use that command.

DIR PRN

This command *prints* the directory listing to an attached printer as well as showing it on the screen.

Wildcards with DIR

You may want to obtain a more *specific directory listing* at times. DOS provides **two** special symbols, called **wildcards**, that allow you to list files with certain attributes. The two wildcard symbols are an **asterisk (*)** and a **question mark (?)**.

The **asterisk (*)** means "any number of characters."

The **question mark (?)** means "any one character."

The two wildcards are used with *partial* filenames. Instead of writing a full filename, you write only part of it and fill in the rest with a wildcard. The following examples will give you a better idea of how the wildcards work with the DIR command.

DIR *.TXT

This command gives you a directory listing of all file names within the current directory that have 'TXT' as their extension name.

DIR INV*.*

This command gives a directory listing of all files in the current directory that begin with "INV."

DIR INVOICE.?

This command gives a directory listing of all files named INVOICE with an extension name that contains only one character.

What Did You Learn?

One of the benefits of a computer system is its ability to store *large amounts* of information. **Organization** becomes essential when working with so much information. To help organize disk drives, your disk operating system allows you to group common types of **information** (files) **into directories.** Directories and files can be identified through names that indicate their contents. If you create logical directories then your work with the computer will be easier and more efficient.

The **path name** for each directory indicates its location within the overall structure on your hard drive. The path is also a convenient way of specifying some of the several DOS commands that allow you to manage your directory system.

We described a few **DOS commands** that enable you to organize and move around directories on your hard drive. Change Directory **(CD)**, Make Directory **(MD)**, Remove Directory **(RD)**, and Directory Listing **(DIR)**, all give you the organizational control you need.

In the next chapter, we move one step deeper into the directory structure: **files.** As there are several commands for managing directories, there are also several commands for managing files.

Chapter 13

Working With Files

Files are really the life-blood of your computer. File storage is the *main purpose* of storage drives. And file organization is the main purpose of directories. **All** of the records, documents, and instructions on your computer are stored in files. Whenever you work on your computer, you will first have to open a file. And, more than likely, you will save the changes you have made in a file after working on your computer.

In this chapter we cover the basics of *managing files* on your hard drive. There are several **DOS commands** that help you manage files. We will cover these commands as well as other topics related to files.

Organizing your computer's files.

Files

Once you have *set up a directory* organizing files on your hard drive, it is important that you maintain it. **Maintaining** and **managing** your hard drive requires keeping files in their appropriate directories, renaming files if necessary, and removing "non-active" files. Non-active files contain information that is considered historical or not used very often. You can store these "non-active" files on a diskette and put them in a safe place to be accessed as you need them.

The *key* to successfully using file management commands, as well as other DOS commands, is to know where you are in your storage drive and where you want to go. **Pathnames, directories,** and *filenames* are very important. Can you imagine your frustration if you had to find a specific document in a filing cabinet that had no organization? *One thing that helps organize files is filenames.*

Filenames

The first thing you notice about a file is its *name*, which consists of *two parts:* the **name** itself and the **extension**. As stated earlier, the actual name can be up to **eight** (8) **characters** long. The extension can be up to **three** (3) **characters** long. An extension name is not mandatory when naming a file. In fact, you may find many files without them.

As a rule, you should give a file a logical name based on its contents. The following are a few examples of filenames and their possible contents.

File name	Possible contents
LTR-MJD.1	First letter to MJD Co.
CONTRACT.MJD	Contract info for MJD Co.
CHAP2	Second chapter of a book
MEMOMISC.DOC	Miscellaneous Memos

Many people and businesses establish *naming standards* for file names. This practice comes in handy when you urgently need to find a file in the computer of a person who is on vacation. If you have file naming standards, then you will know which files might contain the information you are looking for. Some standard examples could be:

All file names containing a letter must have the extension **LTR**. *Example:* THANKS.LTR

All file names containing a memo must have the extension **MEM**.
Example: STATUS.MEM

All files that contain invoice information must begin with **INV** and then the
month and the **year** of the invoice. The file name INV0190 contains all of
the invoices for January of 1990. You could next use the extension name
to number the invoices (i.e., INV0190.**101**).

Keyboard Characters You Can't Use (in a filename)

A filename consist of any character that can be generated from the keyboard
with *a few exceptions.* The following characters **cannot** be used, under any
circumstance, in a filename.

    *** + . " [ ] / \ : < > ; , ? =**

These characters have *special* meaning to DOS. These characters are all
used by DOS to work *other kinds* of magic.

Also... filenames **cannot** contain spaces! This is a common mistake among
filenames (users.)

Extensions

There are a few generally accepted standard extension *(three characters
only)* names.   The standard extension names are as follows:

File Extension	**Probable Contents**
.TXT	Text files
.DOC	Word processing document
.LTR	Letter
.MEM	Memo
.RPT	Report
.EXE	An executable program
.COM	Command
.SYS	A DOS system file

Copying a File (COPY Command)

The COPY command *makes a copy of a file* or group of files from one location to the another. The file you are copying is called the **source** file. The location where you want to move the file to is called the **destination** or target. You can use the COPY command for several purposes:

Move files from one location to the another.

Share information with another computer.

Make a daily **copy** of your information onto a floppy diskette for *safety reasons.*

Make a **copy** of the information onto a diskette for *historical archive purposes.*

What It Looks Like

The COPY command has *three* parts: the **command**, the name of the **source** file, and the name of the **destination** file. The source and destination file names should include the *entire* path for the file. This path includes all directories you need to go through to get to the directory that contains the file. The path also includes the full name of the file, with the extension. You really need to understand your directory structure when copying files.

> ***Example.*** The following examples should give you a better idea of how the COPY command works.

In the first example, we copy a file called "TEMP1.DOC" from the WORD directory on the "C" drive **to** the "A" drive. Once copied to the "A" drive, the file is renamed "TEMP1.BAK".

```
C:\> COPY C:\WORD\TEMP1.DOC A:TEMP1.BAK
```

The COPY command is very helpful in copying files between diskettes. The following example shows how a file named "TEMP2.DOC" is moved from the "B" diskette drive **to** the "A" diskette drive:

```
C:\> COPY B:TEMP2.DOC A:
```

The file keeps its original name since no new name was specified in the command.

Moving A File Using COPY

In managing your storage drive you may find that a specific file or files are in the *wrong* directory. You will want to **move** those files into the correct directory. To move a file to another location, you need to use the **COPY** command with the **DELETE** command. You would first COPY the misplaced file into the correct directory, then DELETE it from the incorrect directory. It is important that you copy the file to its new location and *verify* that it is there *before* you delete it from the original location. The DELETE command is covered later in this chapter.

Using Wildcards with COPY

Wildcards, which we first discussed in chapter 12, are very useful for copying many files at a time. When you specify the **COPY** command with a *filename* and **asterisks**, you can copy all files in a directory from one place to another. For example, if you wanted to copy **all** files in the WORD directory to a floppy diskette in drive "A", you could specify:

```
C:\WORD> COPY *.* A:
```

Instead of specifying every file in the WORD directory, the wildcard, "*.*", allows you to specify all the files at once. As you can see, the wildcards can save you a lot of time when you need to copy many files.

Changing the Name of a File (REName Command)

There will come a time when you will want to change the name of a file. The file content may have changed and you want to reflect that change in its name. At that time you can use use the **REN** (REName) command.

What It Looks Like

The **REN** command works like many file management commands. You first specify the command, REN, then the name of the file you want to rename, and finally the new name for the file. The following command would change the file MEMO.DOC to LETTER.DOC.

```
C:\> REN MEMO.DOC LETTER.DOC
```

If the file whose name you want to change *is not* in the current directory, you gotta specify the drive letter and colon (:) or pathname. However, the new filename doesn't need all that extra information:

```
C:\> REN A:\MEMO.DOC LETTER.DOC
```

The file named MEMO.DOC is on your disk in drive "A". You give it the new name LETTER.DOC by the REN (Rename) command.

Deleting a File (DELete Command)

Get ready. We are about to describe one of the *most feared* DOS commands among new computer users. If you understand the **DELETE** command, however, it should serve only *as an asset* in your work with DOS.

DELETE **erases** the files that you specify. It is *helpful* when you want to clean up clutter on your hard disk. Over time, you may not need some files on your drive. And it is best to erase these files since excess clutter on your system can slow it down.

What It Looks Like

The DELETE command consists of two items: the **command** itself and the
name of the file, *with extension*, that you want to delete. The file name should
include a *path* if you are not already in the directory of the file you want to
delete. DOS can be pretty picky when it comes to the DELETE command.
So you must specify the full name of the file you want to delete. If the
computer cannot find the filename you enter, it will give you an
error message.

The following command erases the file INVOICE.001 from the
current directory:

```
C:\> DEL INVOICE.001
```

If the file you want to delete isn't in the current directory, you *gotta specify*
the drive letter and colon (:) or pathname. The following command deletes
the file FILENAME.TXT that is located in the \WORD\CONTRACT directory
in your "A" drive:

```
C:\> DEL A:\WORD\CONTRACT\FILENAME.EXT
```

Using Wild Cards With DELETE

When you first start using DELETE, avoid using any **wildcard**
(* and ?) symbols. *Wildcards can delete many files at once.* You should have
a good knowledge of wildcard use **before** using them with DELETE.

As you become more skilled in your use of DOS, you may try using wildcards
with DELETE. Since deleting a large number of files is a serious event, the
computer will **always warn you**. If you specified the following command

```
C:\> DEL *.*
```

the computer would return with the question: **Are you sure? (Y/N) :**

DEL *.* *is the most drastic DELETE command you can use.* It **erases** every single file in your current directory. It can be useful if you want to delete an entire directory, but **devastating** to you if you don't. So you should only respond with a **Yes** (Y) if you are sure you want to erase all files. Responding **No** (N) takes you back to the original system prompt.

In general you will only want to use the DELETE command with a wildcard *if:*

You have already **made a copy** of the files somewhere else.

You are sure you **will not** need the files again.

UNDELETE (An Escape Route)

The latest version of DOS, version 5, includes a new command that allows you to **UNDELETE** a file you've just - **Oh No!** - deleted. This command is called, obviously enough, UNDELETE. The UNDELETE command is used the same way as the DELETE command is used. You specify the name and the pathname of the file you want to undelete after the UNDELETE command. *There is a slight catch,* however. You have to specify the UNDELETE command right after specifying the incorrect DELETE command.

UNDELETE will show you the file's name and whether or not it can be undeleted. If it's a go, the system will ask you if you want to UNDELETE the file. Of course you'll answer, **Yes** (Y) or **No** (N). It'll also ask you for the first letter of the filename.

YES, you can also use the UNDELETE command *with wildcards.*

Copying All Files on a Diskette (DISKCOPY Command)

The DISKCOPY command provides a fast way to make a **copy** of files from one diskette to another. *DISKCOPY takes one floppy disk and makes an exact duplicate of it.* DISKCOPY even formats a new disk if it was previously unformatted.

What It Looks Like

When you're copying disks, DOS calls the *original* disk the **source** disk. The disk to which you are *copying to* is referred to as the **target** disk. It's always a good idea to **write-protect** your source (original) disk before you copy it. (Refer to "write-protect" section in chapter 10). The DISKCOPY command includes drive letters for the source and target diskette drives.

The following is a sample of the DISKCOPY command:

> C:\> **DISKCOPY A: B:**

This command copies all files on the diskette in drive "A" to the diskette in drive "B".

> *Examples*. DISKCOPY is uscd differently for systems with **one** and **two** floppy diskette drives. It also requires you to follow *several prompts*. The *first example* describes how to use DISKCOPY with only one diskette drive. The *second example* describes DISKCOPY use with two diskette drives.

> **1) One diskette drive.** Type the following command at the system prompt:

> C:\> **DISKCOPY A: A:**

and press the **ENTER** key.

You will then receive the following prompt:

> *Insert **source** diskette in drive A*
> *Strike any key when ready*

You should then insert the diskette you want to **duplicate** into drive "A" and press any key. The computer fills its memory with as many files as it can and then asks you to:

> *Insert **target** diskette in drive A*
> *Strike any key when ready*

You should take the source diskette out of the drive, then insert the diskette you are **copying files to** (the target diskette).

Depending on how many files you have to copy, the computer may ask you to continue alternately inserting the source and target diskettes. The computer can only copy so many files at a time. So be prepared to know which is the source diskette and which is the target diskette.

2) Two diskette drives. Type the following command at the system prompt:

> C:\> **DISKCOPY A: B:**

and press the Enter key. The computer copies all files from the first drive indicated, to the second drive indicated. In this example, make sure that the diskette you want to duplicate - *the source diskette* - is inserted into drive "A" and the diskette you want to copy the files to - *the target diskette* - is in drive "B".

NOTE: You **cannot** DISKCOPY disks of different size or capacity.

Making a Backup Copy of Your Work (BACKUP Command)

Backing up means to *copy* valuable files on your main storage drive to a removable disk, such as a diskette, that can be stored outside of your system. If your storage drive has trouble (and sometimes they do) you can always rely on your *backup copies*. An efficient back up schedule would include backing up at the end of each day. With such a schedule the largest amount of data you could lose is one day's worth.

What It Looks Like

The BACKUP command mainly includes storage information on the drive and directories that are *copied* and *stored*. The following BACKUP command tells DOS to copy all files in the WORD directory to the diskette in drive "A":

```
C:\> BACKUP C:\WORD A:
```

Example. Like other DOS commands, BACKUP can include pathnames for convenience. BACKUP also contains some options that provide additional features. For example, the following BACKUP command:

```
C:\> BACKUP C:\WORD A:/s
```

will backup all the files in the WORD directory and all the files in the subdirectories of the WORD directory (i.e., LETTERS, CONTRACT, NICAL , MJD) to the diskette in drive "A".

This special subdirectory backup function is requested through the **/s option**. BACKUP has several other options, including the **/w option** that backs up only those files that have changed since the last time you backed up. You can see that the /w can help you save time during your disk backups.

Retrieving Backup Files (RESTORE Command)

The RESTORE command allows you to **recopy** files *originally backed up* using the BACKUP command. You need the restore command if your storage drive goes down and you need access to the files that were copied using the BACKUP command. As long as you have used BACKUP to save these files, you can use RESTORE to put them back. In a sense, this command "restores" your disk drive to its original condition.

What It Looks Like

The RESTORE command is set up nearly **opposite** to the BACKUP command. You specify two drives in the command, but the *first drive* is where your duplicate files are located. The following command would restore files stored on the diskette in drive "A" to your storage drive "C":

```
C:\> RESTORE A: C:
```

Example. The RESTORE command also has several options that add convenience to your file restoration procedure. For example, the following command

```
C:\> RESTORE A: C:/S/P
```

restores all subdirectories (**/s**) and prompts you before restoring files that have been changed since the last backup (**/p**). The following are a few more RESTORE options:

/b:date Restores only those files last modified on or **before** the *specified date.*

/a:date Restores only those files last modified on or **after** the *specified date.*

/m Restores only those files modified since the **last** backup.

<u>What Did You Learn?</u>

Maintaining your storage drive and **managing** your files is just as important as setting the drive up in the first place. You need to be able to find your files when you want to from where you last stored them. So *good file management* practices are essential to successful computing.

DOS provides you with several file *management* commands.

The **COPY** command *copies files* from one part of your directory structure to another.

RENAME allows you to *change the name* of an existing file.

DELETE *erases* a file from a specific location on your hard drive.

UNDELETE is your *escape* to the last deletion you made. And only the last one.

The **DISKCOPY** command *copies* all of the files on a diskette to another diskette.

BACKUP *copies* files for the purpose of storage outside the computer.

RESTORE takes files copied by BACKUP and returns them to their *original* location.

Chapter 14

Laying Out The Buck$

Buying a computer can be *scary*. Even if you are well-informed, there are many things to consider. In this book we've taught you the basic parts of a computer. This should prepare you for talking with computer sales types. The terms **storage**, **memory**, and **monitor** will not be foreign to you when you are searching for your computer. However, there are *other aspects* to consider beyond the technical.

The first thing to remember is that it *pays to research*. Research your own computer needs and the products in which you are interested. In this chapter, we get you started on your research by describing places that sell computers as well as advice you may receive before buying a computer.

Where Do I Buy One?

There is not a generally accepted "best" place to buy a computer. A good starting point is to get **recommendations** from friends or people you know that are knowledgeable of computers. Most major cities have **PC User's groups** that can give valuable insight on buying computers. **Computer magazines** also provide lots of information that allows you to **compare prices** on similar computer systems.

The following sections describe the *different places* that sell computers:

Computer Dealers

A computer dealer is typically a business that sells *computers, software, printers,* and *accessories.* The dealer may also provide *service, training* and other *support.*

Every product has a **suggested retail price** that is set by the product manufacturer. If you are paying that price or close to that price, then you should expect a certain level of *support to be included.* Find out what kind of support is included with your computer and get it in writing. Don't be afraid to ask, "Why should I buy from you?"

Discount dealers usually sell product at *below* suggested retail price. These lower prices will sometimes affect the amount of after-sale support you will get, if any. Again, don't be afraid to ask what kind of support you can expect.

Value Added Reseller (VAR) a.k.a. "Consultant‹

A *value added reseller* (VAR) adds value to each sale in the form of *extra* software, support, or training. You get more than just the computer and the box it comes in.

Typically a VAR specializes in a specific market. They are experts *(or should be)* in their specific market. An example might be a VAR that sells accounting software and computers to doctors' offices. VARs typically sell a complete solution to your computer needs. This solution may include the computer, printer, software, installation of the system, training, warranty and on-going support.

Mail Order Companies (Manufacturer Direct)

Mail order companies have become **very popular** in recent years. Many *well known* hardware and software manufacturers sell directly through mail order to users just like yourself. You do not need to set foot outside your front door to buy a computer through mail order. You will find many reputable mail order companies in all the computer trade magazines. *(Most with toll-free numbers, too!)*

Typically, prices through mail order channels are much lower than going through dealers or VARs. Even though mail order pricing and policies are probably among the most competitive, don't assume that their pricing is the lowest. **Shop around.**

Among the better known mail order companies, **service** and **customer support** are often unmatched since there is usually no one between you and the manufacturer. For instance, some offer **30-day money back guarantees**. Then there is **toll-free telephone support**, 24 hours a day, etc. Definitely some advantages.

A good rule for buying from mail order houses: Make your purchase with a **credit card**. Why? Because if your product is not delivered, or turns up defective, you can contact your credit card company and they'll help you deal with *just about any problems* you might have with these firms. Credit card purchases these days are **excellent protection** against fraud.

Also... some credit card companies will *double your warranty* on purchases made with their credit cards. That's a pretty good deal, *especially* with computers!

Retailers (Warehouse Distributors)

They sell kitchen appliances, stereos, and VCRs, *so why not computers?* Most big retailers - department stores, home shopping clubs, and even some large grocery chains - have gotten into the computer business. Use the **same advice** as with the computer dealers and other computer sellers. *Know what you are looking for.*

In most cases, these type of sales outlets do not specialize in computer sales. So it stands to reason that a big retailer may not have the same knowledge able sales staff that a computer dealer will have. But if you buy from a retailer you can still receive the same quality of support if they're a dealer that is authorized by the manufacturer.

Who Do I Listen To?

Getting advice on how to buy a computer is sort of like getting advice on raising children. *Everyone* has their own opinion on how it should be done.

When obtaining advice, you should realize your particular needs. Not everyone is the same. A business computer user will undoubtedly need different hardware and software than a home computer user. *Ask around*, but always rely on your own choices.

Talk to people who use a computer similar to the way you are going to use one. Ask them *what they like, don't like,* and what they wish they had known before their purchase. You'll learn a lot. We'll cover the advice you are likely to get and our ideas on this advice.

Where You Buy

Advice You'll Get. Buy a computer from a reseller that has a good reputation for service, training and support. Don't let price be your number one consideration. Spending an extra couple hundred dollars initially on support is a lot better than dealing with problems later.

What We Think. We **agree** with this opinion. It is important that you buy a computer from someone you trust and respect. You will need their help if anything goes wrong.

Specialized Dealers

Advice You'll get. If you are going to be doing something *very specialized* with your system, you will want to work with a reseller who is an expert in that area and sells specialized software. These resellers are usually called Value Added Resellers (VARs).

What We Think. There are a lot of "off the shelf" software packages that can apply to a lot of different types of businesses. However, if you need one that is very specific, *you should* talk to a specialist. Often a specialist can also tell you how to use more popular software packages for your particular needs. Again, make sure the VAR is a *reputable business.* You may have to pay a little more for their expertise, but it's worth it.

How Advanced a Computer?

Advice You'll Get. Computer technology advances so fast that you should get the top of the line now so that in a couple of years your computer isn't out of date.

What We Think. Computer technology *does* advance very quickly, but that does not mean you should buy the top of the line all the time. New technology is usually *over-priced* and sometimes *unproven* when it is first introduced. You should get a computer that can solve the problems you have today and handle your expected growth for the next 2-3 years. Get a system that can grow as your needs grow. You should be able to add more storage, memory, software, and even a better monitor to your system.

Price, How Much Should I Pay?

Advice You'll Get. Go for low price and don't worry about support. Most resellers can help if something in your system goes wrong.

What We Think. Picture This: You have been working on a 300 page report that is due tomorrow. You can't get it to print and you don't know what is wrong. The place that you bought it from went out of business a week after you bought your system.

Do you see how support and quality become a concern? The lowest price in town does not mean the best buy. You should look at the company, the quality of its product, and the service you can expect after the sale.

Talking To a Consultant

Advice You'll Get. Go to a computer consultant and pay them to analyze your computer needs and budget.

What We Think. Using a knowledgeable consultant's advice can be an excellent idea. Identifying your needs and fitting that with your budget is not always an easy task. Finding someone to help you is a good idea. Computer sales representatives are usually paid for selling you a computer. Finding the right computer for your needs and budget may not be the primary concern of many computer sales people.

What Did You Learn?

Purchasing a computer is an investment decision you should not take lightly. When purchasing a car you typically look at the quality and after-purchase service that you will receive. You should observe the same care when purchasing a computer.

There are a lot of computers made by many different manufac turers and these computers are sold by even more computer resellers. The bottom line is to determine your computer needs, the amount of support you need, and how much you are willing to pay. Remember, if you will only accept a "rock bottom" price, you can probably assume that the level of support will also be "rock bottom."

Glossary

Computer talk. The only thing **worse** than trying to understand computer talk is trying to understand the instructions to your VCR. I *personally* think you have a better shot at understanding computer talk.

In the computer world, you'll find words in computer books that you just don't understand. Fortunately, *it ain't critical* that you learn them all. But there are a few terms you may want to learn in the event you go shopping for a

computer *or* if you find yourself in the middle of a conversation with a bunch of computer nerds. You wouldn't want to have that "Huh?" look on your face now, would you?

Adapter Cards

Also referred to as "expansion cards". They are electronic circuit boards that attach to your computer's insides (see Expansion Slots). They allow you to "add" other features to your computer that it may not have originally come with.

Application Software

Application software is a general term for programs that tell the computer to do a specific function. Software specific to writing would be a word processing application software. Other examples of application software would be spreadsheet, desktop publishing, etc.

ASCII

Short for "American Standard Code for Information Interchange". Pronounced "ASK-ee", this is a character (letters, symbols and other non-numerical data) coding system most commonly used by computers. Computers can only process numerical information. ASCII converts numerical values (numbers) to characters and digits that us humans can understand. For example, the letter "A" is represented by the number 65 in ASCII Code.

Backup

A backup is an additional copy of work done on the computer that is stored outside the computer for safe keeping. You can back up information by using the BACKUP, COPY, or DISKCOPY commands.

BIOS

Short for "Basic Input Output System". The computers self-check system. Instructions for the basic operation of the computer hardware stored in the ROM (Read Only Memory) chip. You may hear the two terms combined as the ROM BIOS.

Bit

Short for **BI**nary digi**T**, this is the smallest unit of information handled by a computer. A bit is either 0 (off) or 1 (on) and is represented by a single electronic pulse. Forget it! Just remember that 8 (eight) bits equal 1 (one) byte and that 1 byte is equal to 1 character (letter, number, symbol or punctuation mark).

Boot

Computer slang for starting the computer. When you initially turn a computer on, you are "booting" it up. Resetting the computer is called "re-booting" or "warm boot".

Byte

Bytes are units of measurement for computer storage. A group of 8 (eight) bits is equal to 1 (one) byte. 1 byte is equal to 1 character (letter, number, symbol or punctuation mark). See kilobyte and megabyte.

Compatibility

Capable of existing in harmony. The hardware and software of your system must be compatible if they are to work together. If they are compatible that means they were design to work with that type of computer and/or software.

CPU

Short for central processing unit. This is sometimes used as the term for the main box of the computer. It holds all of the electronics and computer chips. We look at it as the "brains" of the computer.

CPS

Stands for characters per second. A key measurement for the speed of a dot matrix printer.

Chip

Also known as a computer chip, micro chip, or processor chip. Chips contain complex circuitry that contain instructions to do a specific function. Memory chips store information and processor chips process information.

Command

An instruction to the computer telling it to perform a specific function. The Enter key is mostly used to *issue* commands.

Cursor

A blinking underline or flashing dash symbol that indicates where you are on the screen. It is the location where the next command or piece of information will be entered. A cursor can be a dash, rectangle, or an arrow symbol.

Date Base

A collection of files grouped together into similar information. You can sort this information in many different ways. If you get "junk mail" then your name and address is most likely on a data base mailing list.

Directory

A directory can be created on your storage drive as a method of organizing your information. You can organize each group of similar information into directories so you can find them easier. Examples include creating a directory that contains only accounting information and another separate directory containing only your writing information.

Disk

An electronically encoded recording removable media for storing information. There are three types of disks: floppy disks (5 1/4-inch and 3 1/2-inch), hard disks, and optical disks. These devices store computer information.

DOS

Stands for Disk Operating System. This is a type of software called operating system software that is used in most IBM or IBM compatible computers. Every computer must have some type of operating system software. It is the manager of the interaction between humans and parts of the computer. It provides you with the "maintenance" commands to manage the information stored on your computer as well as set up your computer to make computing easier.

Dot Matrix Printer

A type of printer that creates the characters by the different formation of pins pressed onto an ink ribbon. It got its name from the fact the characters are created by ink dots.

Diskette

Another name for disk. A form of removable storage media. Also termed a floppy disk.

Display

Where you see what is happening, the computer's way of communicating with you. Also known as a video display, terminal, screen, or monitor. Like televisions, you can have a color or monochrome (one color) display

EGA

Stands for Enhanced Graphics Adapter. A level of quality in a color monitor and video adapter card. Now replaced in quality by the VGA quality.

Expansion Card

These are electronic circuit boards that attach themselves to the inside of your computer to *expansion slots.* These let you expand the capabilities of your computer by allowing you to add extra devices.

Expansion Slot

Allows you to expand the capability of what your computer can do by inserting expansion cards. Expansion slots are located on the mother board and most systems have room for about six to eight cards.

File

A form in which the computer stores information. A file can contain written information, numbers, or programming instructions. Each file has a uniquely identifiable name assigned to it.

Floppy Disk

A type of removable disk using flexible media. They can come in 5 1/4-inch and 3 1/2-inch sizes.

Font

A specific "look" of a printed character. Each font style has a unique name so you can request in by name. You use font styles to give a unique look to a printed page.

Format

Preparing storage media to accept the storage of information. It also sets up the media to recognize the operating system software that you computer is using. All storage media must be formatted before it is used for the first time. Formatting will erase all information previously on the media.

Function Keys

The 12 keys across the top of the keyboard, labeled F1 through F12. These could be considered "short cut" keys. They are used by software programs to complete a specific function with only one keystroke rather than what could have taken many. Their individual functions are determined by the software.

Graphics

The capability of the monitor to display graphs, charts, and drawings. A computer and monitor without graphics capabilities will only display text.

GUI

Stands for Graphic User Interface. Allows the users to point to a list of commands or pictures that represent commands rather than typing a character based command. You typically point with a device called a mouse.

Hard Disk

Rigid *non-removable* storage disks that can store much more information than a diskette. Used for long term storage and provides faster access to your computer information.

Hardware

The components of the computer system that you can touch and feel. Much like a cassette player that plays music; the cassette player is the *hardware* and the cassette tape is the *software*. Software controls the hardware. Hardware examples include **monitors, keyboards, mouse,** etc.

K or Kb

Stands for kilobyte. See kilobyte.

Keyboard

The combination of typewriter like keyboard, plus the numeric key pad, cursor control keys and function keys. This device allows you to communicate with your computer to input information and commands.

Kilobyte

A term used for measuring storage capacity on computer disks (hard and floppy disks) and chips. **1 kilobyte** is equal to 1,024 bytes (this number is usually rounded off to 1,000 bytes in computer circles) of information equal to *about 1/2 page of text.*

Laser Printer

A high quality printer that uses a laser beam to make the image on the paper. It acts and looks much like a copy machine. Quiet and fast and expensive. Produces great graphics.

LED

Light emitting diode. A light display indicating whether a specific function or capability is on or off. You will find an LED indicating whether the power to your computer is on or off.

Mb

Stands for megabyte. See Megabyte

MHz

This stands for megahertz. This refers to how *fast* a computer can think. Computer speeds range from 4.77 MHz to 66 MHz. The difference in those speeds would be like going cross country in a **volkswagen** (4.77 MHz) or a **jet** (66 MHz). They'll both ultimately get you there but at different times.

Microprocessor

It's what we refer to as the "brains" of the computer. It's where all the "thinking" gets done. They are also called CPU's or processors. You'll hear them called by numbers they've been given by the makers of these things, numbers like 386 and 486.

Megabyte

Another term used for measuring storage capacity on computer storage disks and chips. **1 megabyte** is equal to 1,048,576 bytes (round this one off to a million bytes for simplicity) of information. That's equal to about 500 pages of text.

Memory

The storage capacity of the computer. See RAM and ROM.

Menu

The listing of programs and function options displayed on the computer's screen. You can then choose what you want to do by indicating which item from the list you want.

Modem

A device that allows computers to send and receive information over telephone lines.

Monitor

See Display.

Motherboard

The big green circuit board inside the computer. It is the computer's main location of circuitry. Every part of the computer is somehow connected to the motherboard. It contains the processor chip, memory chips, expansion slots and other circuitry.

Mouse

A hand held pointing device that allows you to communicate with the computer. Typically used with GUI type software (see GUI).

Parallel Port

A port that enables the computer to communicate with a external device that can send and accept parallel communication. Parallel communication means that information is sent 8 bits or 1 byte at a time.

Path Name

The set of directions through the established directory organization to get the information you are looking for. An example: to get to the INVOICE directory the path name would be C:>ACCOUNT\INVOICE.

PC

Stands for personal computer.

Port

A "hole in the back of the computer" that allows you to attach various outside things. (Like printers.) These holes or ports allow communication of information to and from the computer and its external devices.

Printer

The output device that provides you with a printed copy of information from the computer. You need a printer to get the information inside of your computer onto "hard copy."

Prompt

The prompt is the computers way of telling you what drive you are on and that it is ready to accept a command. An example would be **C:\>** which indicates you are accessing the "C" storage drive.

RAM

Stands for random access memory. This is the computers temporary storage memory. Information is stored on computer memory chips. Everything in RAM is lost when the computer is turned off unless you have first saved to a storage drive. Information in RAM can be accessed very quickly.

ROM

Stands for read only memory. A computer chip where the computer stores valuable information only the manufacturer can change. The computer can only read the information but can't change it.

Serial Port

A port that enables the computer to communicate with a external device that can send and accept serial communication. Serial communication means that information is sent one bit at a time.

Software

A set of pre-defined instructions that tell the computer to perform specific tasks, i.e. word processing, accounting, games. Basically, it "bosses" the hardware (computer) around. It's the reason we have computers.

Spreadsheet

A software program that simulates an accountant's worksheet, designed to manipulate numbers.

System

A completely set up computer system. This would include the computer, monitor, printer, and software.

VGA

Stands for video graphics array. A level of quality in a color monitor and video adapter card. Offers great color and resolution. Probably the best buy for monitors these days.

Word Processing

A software program that allows you to write, edit and print documents.

Write Protect

A way to *prevent* the accidental writing, changing, or erasing of information on the diskette. 5 1/4-inch diskettes can be write protected by covering the write protect notch with a sticky tab and the 3 1/2-inch diskettes can be write protected by sliding the write protect tab so that the hole is showing through.

WYSIWYG

Stands for *what-you-see-is-what-you-get.* It means that if you software program has the capabilities, what you see on the screen will be printed out exactly (or close to it) as you see it on the screen. It doesn't always work, but that's the general idea.